# interchange

## FOURTH EDITION

## Jack C. Richards

With Jonathan Hull and Susan Proctor

Series Editor: David Bohlke

CAMBRIDGE
UNIVERSITY PRESS

STUDENT'S BOOK

3B

# CAMBRIDGE
## UNIVERSITY PRESS

University Printing House, Cambridge CB2 8BS, United Kingdom

One Liberty Plaza, 20th Floor, New York, NY 10006, USA

477 Williamstown Road, Port Melbourne, VIC 3207, Australia

4843/24, 2nd Floor, Ansari Road, Daryaganj, Delhi – 110002, India

79 Anson Road, #06–04/06, Singapore 079906

Cambridge University Press is part of the University of Cambridge.

It furthers the University's mission by disseminating knowledge in the pursuit of education, learning and research at the highest international levels of excellence.

www.cambridge.org
Information on this title: www.cambridge.org/9781107652699

First published 1998
Third edition 2005
20  19  18  17  16  15  14  13  12  11  10  9  8  7  6

Printed in the United Kingdom by Latimer Trend

*A catalogue record for this publication is available from the British Library*

ISBN 978-1-107-64870-8 Student's Book 3 with Self-study DVD-ROM
ISBN 978-1-107-69720-1 Student's Book 3A with Self-study DVD-ROM
ISBN 978-1-107-65269-9 Student's Book 3B with Self-study DVD-ROM
ISBN 978-1-107-64874-6 Workbook 3
ISBN 978-1-107-64685-8 Workbook 3A
ISBN 978-1-107-68752-3 Workbook 3B
ISBN 978-1-107-61506-9 Teacher's Edition 3 with Assessment Audio CD/CD-ROM
ISBN 978-1-107-66870-6 Class Audio 3 CDs
ISBN 978-1-107-66684-9 Full Contact 3 with Self-study DVD-ROM
ISBN 978-1-107-62042-1 Full Contact 3A with Self-study DVD-ROM
ISBN 978-1-107-63667-5 Full Contact 3B with Self-study DVD-ROM

For a full list of components, visit www. cambridge.org/interchange

Art direction, book design, layout services, and photo research: Integra
Audio production: CityVox, NYC
Video production: Nesson Media Boston, Inc.

# Welcome to *Interchange Fourth Edition*, the world's most successful English series!

*Interchange* offers a complete set of tools for learning how to communicate in English.

## Student's Book
### with NEW Self-study DVD-ROM

- **Complete video program** with additional **video exercises**

- Additional **vocabulary**, **grammar, speaking**, **listening**, and **reading** practice
- Printable **score reports** to submit to teachers

## Available online

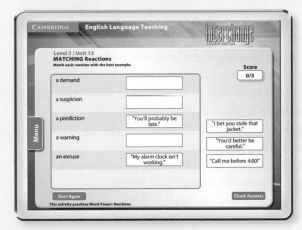

### *Interchange* Arcade

- **Free** self-study website
- **Fun**, interactive, self-scoring activities
- Practice **vocabulary**, **grammar**, **listening**, and **reading**
- **MP3s** of the class audio program

### Online Workbook

- A variety of **interactive activities** that correspond to each Student's Book lesson
- **Instant feedback** for hundreds of activities
- **Easy to use** with clear, easy-to-follow instructions
- Extra **listening practice**
- Simple tools for teachers to **monitor progress** such as scores, attendance, and time spent online

# Authors' acknowledgments

A great number of people contributed to the development of *Interchange Fourth Edition*. Particular thanks are owed to the reviewers using *Interchange*, *Third Edition* in the following schools and institutes – their insights and suggestions have helped define the content and format of the fourth edition:

Ian Geoffrey Hanley, **The Address Education Center**, Izmir, Turkey

James McBride, **AUA Language Center**, Bangkok, Thailand

Jane Merivale, **Centennial College**, Toronto, Ontario, Canada

Elva Elena Peña Andrade, **Centro de Auto Aprendizaje de Idiomas**, Nuevo León, Mexico

José Paredes, **Centro de Educación Continua de la Escuela Politécnica Nacional** (CEC-EPN), Quito, Ecuador

Chia-jung Tsai, **Changhua University of Education**, Changhua City, Taiwan

Kevin Liang, **Chinese Culture University**, Taipei, Taiwan

Roger Alberto Neira Perez, **Colegio Santo Tomás de Aquino**, Bogotá, Colombia

Teachers at **Escuela Miguel F. Martínez**, Monterrey, Mexico

Maria Virgínia Goulart Borges de Lebron, **Great Idiomas**, São Paulo, Brazil

Gina Kim, **Hoseo University**, Chungnam, South Korea

Heeyong Kim, Seoul, South Korea

Elisa Borges, **IBEU-Rio**, Rio de Janeiro, Brazil

Jason M. Ham, **Inha University**, Incheon, South Korea

Rita de Cássia S. Silva Miranda, **Instituto Batista de Idiomas**, Belo Horizonte, Brazil

Teachers at **Instituto Politécnico Nacional**, Mexico City, Mexico

Victoria M. Roberts and Regina Marie Williams, **Interactive College of Technology**, Chamblee, Georgia, USA

Teachers at **Internacional de Idiomas**, Mexico City, Mexico

Marcelo Serafim Godinho, **Life Idiomas**, São Paulo, Brazil

J. Kevin Varden, **Meiji Gakuin University**, Yokohama, Japan

Rosa Maria Valencia Rodríguez, Mexico City, Mexico

Chung-Ju Fan, **National Kinmen Institute of Technology**, Kinmen, Taiwan

Shawn Beasom, **Nihon Daigaku**, Tokyo, Japan

Gregory Hadley, **Niigata University of International and Information Studies**, Niigata, Japan

Chris Ruddenklau, **Osaka University of Economics and Law**, Osaka, Japan

Byron Roberts, **Our Lady of Providence Girls' High School**, Xindian City, Taiwan

Simon Banha, **Phil Young's English School**, Curitiba, Brazil

Flávia Gonçalves Carneiro Braathen, **Real English Center**, Viçosa, Brazil

Márcia Cristina Barboza de Miranda, **SENAC**, Recife, Brazil

Raymond Stone, **Seneca College of Applied Arts and Technology**, Toronto, Ontario, Canada

Gen Murai, **Takushoku University**, Tokyo, Japan

Teachers at **Tecnológico de Estudios Superiores de Ecatepec**, Mexico City, Mexico

Teachers at **Universidad Autónoma Metropolitana–Azcapotzalco**, Mexico City, Mexico

Teachers at **Universidad Autónoma de Nuevo León**, Monterrey, Mexico

Mary Grace Killian Reyes, **Universidad Autónoma de Tamaulipas**, Tampico Tamaulipas, Mexico

Teachers at **Universidad Estatal del Valle de Ecatepec**, Mexico City, Mexico

Teachers at **Universidad Nacional Autónoma de Mexico – Zaragoza**, Mexico City, Mexico

Teachers at **Universidad Nacional Autónoma de Mexico – Iztacala**, Mexico City, Mexico

Luz Edith Herrera Diaz, Veracruz, Mexico

Seri Park, **YBM PLS**, Seoul, South Korea

**Self-assessment** charts revised by Alex Tilbury
**Grammar plus** written by Karen Davy

# Plan of Book 3B

| Titles/Topics | Speaking | Grammar |
|---|---|---|
| **UNIT 9**      PAGES 58–63 | | |
| **Improvements**<br>Everyday services; recommendations; self-improvement | Talking about things you need to have done; asking for and giving advice or suggestions | Get or have something done; making suggestions with modals + verbs, gerunds, negative questions, and infinitives |
| **UNIT 10**      PAGES 64–69 | | |
| **The past and the future**<br>Historic events and people; biography; the future | Talking about history events; talking about things to be accomplished in the future | Referring to time in the past with adverbs and prepositions: *during, in, ago, from…to, for, since*; predicting the future with *will*, future continuous, and future perfect |
| PROGRESS CHECK      PAGES 70–71 | | |
| **UNIT 11**      PAGES 72–77 | | |
| **Life's little lessons**<br>Milestones and turning points; behavior and personality; regrets | Describing rites of passage; describing turning points; describing regrets and hypothetical situations | Time clauses: *before, after, once, the moment, as soon as, until, by the time*; expressing regret with *should (not) have* + past participle; describing hypothetical situations with *if* clauses + past perfect |
| **UNIT 12**      PAGES 78–83 | | |
| **The right stuff**<br>Qualities for success; successful businesses; advertising | Describing qualities for success; describing features; giving reasons for success; interviewing for a job; talking about ads and slogans | Describing purpose with infinitive clauses and infinitive clauses with *for*; giving reasons with *because, since, because of, for, due to*, and *the reason* |
| PROGRESS CHECK      PAGES 84–85 | | |
| **UNIT 13**      PAGES 86–91 | | |
| **That's a possibility.**<br>Pet peeves; unexplained events; reactions; complicated situations and advice | Making conclusions; offering explanations; describing hypothetical events; giving advice for complicated situations | Past modals for degrees of certainty: *must (not) have, may (not) have, might (not) have, could (not) have*; past modals for judgments and suggestions: *should (not) have, could (not) have, would (not) have* |
| **UNIT 14**      PAGES 92–97 | | |
| **Behind the scenes**<br>How a movie is made; media professions; processes; the entertainment industry | Describing how something is done or made; describing careers in the media | The passive to describe process with *is/are* + past participle and modal + *be* + past participle; defining and non-defining relative clauses |
| PROGRESS CHECK      PAGES 98–99 | | |
| **UNIT 15**      PAGES 100–105 | | |
| **There should be a law!**<br>Recommendations; opinions; local concerns; controversial issues | Giving opinions for and against controversial issues; offering a different opinion; agreeing and disagreeing | Giving recommendations and opinions with passive modals: *should be, ought to be, must be, has to be, has got to be*; tag questions for opinions |
| **UNIT 16**      PAGES 106–111 | | |
| **Challenges and accomplishments**<br>Challenges; accomplishments; goals; volunteering | Describing challenges, frustrations, and rewards; talking about the past and the future | Complex noun phrases containing gerunds; accomplishments with the present perfect and simple past; goals with the future perfect and *would like to have* + past participle |
| PROGRESS CHECK      PAGES 112–113 | | |
| GRAMMAR PLUS      PAGES 140–147, 150–151 | | |

# 9 Improvements

## 1 SNAPSHOT

**Nine commonly offered services**

- Language tutoring ▷
- Computer services ▷
- House cleaning ▷
- Home repairs ▷
- Moving services ▷
- Financial services ▷
- Music lessons ▷
- Pet-sitting ▷
- Clothing alterations ▷

Source: Based on information from the community bulletin board at the Coffee Pot, New York City

*Why would someone need these services? Have you ever used any of them?*
*What are some other common services and skills people offer?*

## 2 PERSPECTIVES

**A** ▷ Listen to an advertisement. Would you use a service like this?
Why or why not?

**Hazel's Personal Services**

Don't have time to do all the things you need to do? Call Hazel's Personal Services!

- Get your apartment cleaned.
- Have your car washed.
- Get your computer fixed.
- And much more . . . all for a very low price!

Call Hazel! (646) 555-2121

If Hazel doesn't offer the service you need, she'll find someone who does. Guaranteed!

*Hazel offers:*
- Computer support
- Repairs
- Beauty services
- Financial services
- Laundry and dry cleaning
- Pet-sitting

**B** What services do you need or want? What questions would you ask Hazel?

> ## Get or have something done ⓓ
>
> *Use **get** or **have**, the object, and the past participle of the verb to describe a service performed for you by someone else.*
>
> | **Do something yourself** | **Get/have something done for you** |
> | --- | --- |
> | I **clean** my apartment every week. | I **get** my apartment **cleaned** (by Hazel) every week. |
> | He **is washing** his car. | He **is having** his car **washed**. |
> | They **fixed** their computer. | They **got** their computer **fixed**. |
> | Did you **repair** your watch? | Did you **have** your watch **repaired**? |
> | Where can I **print** these pictures? | Where can I **get** these pictures **printed**? |

**A** Complete the sentences to express that the services are performed by someone else.

1. Luis didn't mow the lawn in front of his house. He ___had it mowed___ . (have)
2. Samantha isn't cutting her own hair. She _____ . (get)
3. Barbara doesn't clean her apartment. She _____ . (have)
4. JoAnn and John didn't paint their house. They _____ . (get)
5. Doug isn't repairing his bike. He _____ . (have)

**B** **PAIR WORK** Take turns describing the services in the pictures.

**1. Mei-ling**

**2. Rodrigo**

**3. Maggie**

**4. Simon**

"Mei-ling is getting her skirt shortened."

**C** **PAIR WORK** Tell your partner about three things you've had done for you recently. Ask and answer questions for more information.

**A** ⓓ Listen and practice. Notice that when the object becomes a pronoun (sentence B), it is no longer stressed.

A: Where can I get my **watch fixed**?

B: You can get it **fixed** at the **Time** Shop.

A: Where can I have my **shoes shined**?

B: You can have them **shined** at **Sunshine** Shoes.

**B** **GROUP WORK** Ask questions about three things you want to have done. Pay attention to sentence stress. Other students give answers.

## 5 DISCUSSION  Different places, different ways

**GROUP WORK**  Are these services available in your country? For those that aren't, do you think they would be a good idea?

*Can you . . . ?*

have your portrait drawn by a street artist
get your blood pressure checked at a pharmacy
have your clothes dry-cleaned at work
get library books delivered to your home
have your shoes shined on the street
get your car washed for less than $15
have a suit made in under 24 hours
get your teeth whitened
have pizza delivered after midnight

A:  Can you have your portrait drawn by a street artist?
B:  Sure! You can have it done at . . .

## 6 INTERCHANGE 9  Put yourself in my shoes!

What do teenagers worry about? Go to Interchange 9 on page 123.

## 7 WORD POWER  Three-word phrasal verbs

**A**  Match each phrasal verb in these sentences with its meaning. Then compare with a partner.

**Phrasal verbs**

1. Jennifer has **broken up with** her boyfriend – again! ..........
2. Kevin **came up with** a great idea for our class reunion. ..........
3. I'm not **looking forward to** watching my neighbor's dogs. They're not very friendly. ..........
4. My doctor says I'm overweight. I should **cut down on** fatty foods. ..........
5. Rob can't **keep up with** the students in his Mandarin class. He should get a tutor. ..........
6. I can't **put up with** the noise on my street! I'll have to move. ..........
7. My girlfriend doesn't **get along with** her roommate. They're always fighting. ..........
8. Bill can't **take care of** his own finances. He has an accountant manage his money. ..........

**Meanings**

a.  be excited for
b.  end a romantic relationship with
c.  stay in pace with
d.  tolerate
e.  reduce the quantity of
f.  have a good relationship with
g.  be responsible for
h.  think of; develop

**B  PAIR WORK**  Take turns making sentences with each phrasal verb in part A.

## 8 CONVERSATION *I have two left feet!*

**A** ▶ Listen and practice.

James: This is so depressing! I haven't had a date since Angela broke up with me. What can I do?

Mike: Why don't you join an online dating service? That's how I met Amy.

James: Actually, I've tried that. But the people you meet are always different from what you expect.

Mike: Well, what about taking a dance class? A friend of mine met his wife that way.

James: A dance class? Are you serious?

Mike: Sure, why not? They offer them here at the gym.

James: I don't think that's a very good idea. Have you ever seen me dance? I have two left feet!

**B** **CLASS ACTIVITY** What are some other good ways to meet people?

## 9 GRAMMAR FOCUS

> ### Making suggestions ▶
>
> **With modals + verbs**
> **Maybe you could go** to a chat room.
>
> **With gerunds**
> **What about taking** a dance class?
> **Have you thought about asking** your friends
> to introduce you to their other friends?
>
> **With negative questions**
> **Why don't you join** an online dating service?
>
> **With infinitives**
> **One option is to join** a club.
> **It might be a good idea to check out** those
> discussion groups at the bookstore.

**A** Circle the correct answers. Then practice with a partner.

1. A: How can I build self-confidence?
   B: **What about / Why don't you** participating in more social activities?

2. A: What could help me be happier?
   B: **Maybe / One option** you could try not to get annoyed about little things.

3. A: How can I get better grades?
   B: **Have you thought about / It might be a good idea** to join a study group.

4. A: What can I do to save money?
   B: **Why don't you / What about** come up with a budget?

5. A: How can I get along with my roommate better?
   B: **Why don't you / Have you thought about** planning fun activities to look forward
   to every week?

**B** **GROUP WORK** Take turns asking and answering the questions in part A.
Answer with your own suggestions.

**LISTENING** *All you have to do is . . .*

**A** ▶ Listen to people give different suggestions for each problem.
Put a line through the suggestion that was *not* given.

1. How to overcome shyness:
   a. read a self-help book
   b. join a club
   c. see a therapist
   d. take medication

2. How to stop biting
   your fingernails:
   a. count instead
   b. wear gloves
   c. paint your nails
   d. figure out why you're
      nervous

3. How to organize your
   busy schedule:
   a. program your phone
   b. make a list of priorities
   c. cancel appointments
   d. talk to a consultant

**B** **PAIR WORK** Look at the suggestions. Which one seems the
most helpful? Why?

## 11 SPEAKING *Bad habits*

**GROUP WORK** Make three suggestions for how to break each of these bad habits. Then share
your ideas with the class. Which ideas are the most creative?

*How can I stop . . . ?*

**buying things I don't need**

**eating junk food at night**

**cracking my knuckles**

"One thing you could do is cut up your credit cards. And why don't you . . . ?"

## 12 WRITING *A letter of advice*

**A** Imagine you are an advice columnist at a magazine. Choose one of
the letters below and make a list of suggestions. Then write a reply.

My best friend seems anxious a lot. She bites
her fingernails and always looks tired. I don't
think she's eating right, either. How can I
convince her to take better care of herself?
– *Worried*

I argue with my girlfriend all the time. I try
to do nice things for her, but we always end
up in a fight. I can't put up with this much
longer – what can I do?
– *Frustrated*

**B** **GROUP WORK** Take turns reading your advice. Whose advice do you think will work? Why?

# Critical Thinking

*Have you ever said something – and then regretted that you didn't think carefully before opening your mouth? What happened?*

**1** "Think before you speak!" Has anyone ever said that to you? It's only human to react quickly and perhaps emotionally to things that happen. But without giving ourselves sufficient thinking time, we may see things in terms of black and white instead of considering various shades of gray or other colors. Also, it's all too easy to ignore connections and consequences.

**2** At one level, thinking is fairly simple. For instance, it might simply involve making a shopping list. However, there is a deeper and more complex level of thinking. This is often called "critical thinking," and it has several characteristics. First, it requires that you rely on reason rather than emotion. This means you have to look objectively at all available

evidence and decide if it is true, false, or perhaps partly true. Second, you have to be self-aware and recognize your biases and prejudices because these may cause you to think subjectively. A third characteristic is that you need to be open to new ideas and interpretations.

**3** Critical thinking can help you in just about everything you do. One of the most important things it helps you do is solve problems. This has always been an asset in many traditional fields, such as education, research, business and management. But it's also very useful to help people keep up with the new, fast-moving knowledge economy, which is driven by information and technology. Modern workers often have to analyze and integrate information from many different sources in order to solve problems.

**4** We all sometimes speak before we think, and we all have blind spots. Nevertheless, while thinking critically doesn't always happen automatically, it will certainly serve you well whatever you do in life.

**A**  Read the article. Then write the number of each paragraph next to its main idea.

........... For many people, critical thinking is useful in the workplace.
........... It's worth the effort to think critically.
........... We often don't allow ourselves enough time to think.
........... Critical thinking has three important aspects.

**B**  Read about these people. Which of the three characteristics of critical thinking did they need to apply? Explain your answers.

a = Check if the evidence is true.    b = Recognize your prejudices.    c = Be open to new ideas.

........... 1. Jane worked as a bank teller for ten years. She never considered doing anything else. When she was offered a promotion, she refused it.
........... 2. Bella received an email from someone she didn't know. The email said she had won $1 million in the lottery. She immediately bought a new car.
........... 3. Ian thinks our new neighbors are loud, but I disagree. I think he's just more sensitive to the noise because they play music and watch TV shows that aren't in English.

**C**  **GROUP WORK**  How good are you at critical thinking? How has it helped you?

# 10 The past and the future

## 1 SNAPSHOT

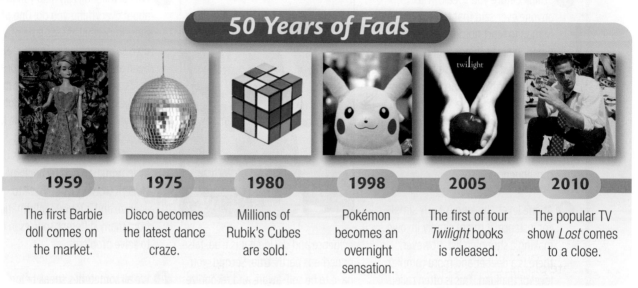

**50 Years of Fads**

| 1959 | 1975 | 1980 | 1998 | 2005 | 2010 |
|------|------|------|------|------|------|
| The first Barbie doll comes on the market. | Disco becomes the latest dance craze. | Millions of Rubik's Cubes are sold. | Pokémon becomes an overnight sensation. | The first of four *Twilight* books is released. | The popular TV show *Lost* comes to a close. |

Sources: *New York Public Library Book of Chronologies;* http://answers.yahoo.com

Have any of these fads ever been popular in your country?
Can you think of four other fads from the past or present?
Is there anything popular right now that could be a fad?

## 2 CONVERSATION *I'm good at history.*

**A** ▶ Listen and practice.

Emma: Look. Here's a quiz on events of the twentieth century.
Steve: Oh, let me give it a try. I'm good at history.
Emma: All right. First question: When did World War I begin?
Steve: I think it began in 1917.
Emma: Huh. And how long has the United Nations been in existence?
Steve: Uh, since Kennedy became president in 1961.
Emma: Hmm. Next question: How long were the Beatles together?
Steve: Well, they started in 1965, and broke up in 1980, so they were together for 15 years. So, how am I doing so far?
Emma: Not very well. Not one of your answers is correct!

**B** ▶ Do you know the answers to the three questions in part A? Listen to the rest of the conversation. What are the correct answers?

# 3 GRAMMAR FOCUS

## Referring to time in the past ▶

**A point or period of time in the past**
When did World War II take place?
**During** the 1940s. **In** the 1940s. Over 70 years **ago**.

How long were the Beatles together?
**From** 1960 **to** 1970. **For** ten years.

**A period of time that continues into the present**
How long has the United Nations been in existence?
**Since** 1945. **Since** World War II ended. **For** about the last 70 years.

**A** Complete the paragraphs with the **boldface** words from the grammar box. Then compare with a partner.

1. The planet Pluto was discovered ...................... 1930. Scientists accepted this ...................... many years but ...................... the 1970s, some began to question if Pluto was indeed a planet. ...................... 2008, after a long debate, Pluto was downgraded to a new category called "dwarf planet." ...................... that time, our solar system has had only eight planets.

2. Scientists found a new species of dinosaur in the U.S. state of Utah ...................... 2007. Like some other species of dinosaur, it ate plants. Unlike other species, however, it had 15 giant horns on its head. These dinosaurs lived ...................... over 30 million years ...................... the Cretaceous period. Scientists believe they lived ............... about 68 ...................... 99 million years ..................

**B** **GROUP WORK** Write two true and two false statements about world events. Then take turns reading your statements. Others give correct information for the false statements.

A: Bill Clinton was president of the U.S. for four years.
B: That's false. He was president for eight years.

# 4 PRONUNCIATION *Syllable stress*

**A** ▶ Listen and practice. Notice which syllable has the main stress in these four- and five-syllable words. Notice the secondary stress.

| appreciate |
| assassination |
| catastrophe |
| consideration |
| conversation |
| revolution |

○●○○
identify

○○●○
disadvantage

○ ○○●○
communication

.................................

.................................

.................................

.................................

.................................

.................................

**B** ▶ Listen to the words in the box. Which syllable has the main stress? Write the words in the correct column in part A.

*The past and the future* ▪ **65**

## 5 WORD POWER Historic events

**A** Match each word with the best example. Then compare with a partner.

1. achievement ............
2. assassination ............
3. discovery ............
4. election ............
5. epidemic ............
6. natural disaster ............
7. revolution ............
8. terrorist act ............

a. The eruption of Mount St. Helens in 1980 destroyed over 250 homes.
b. In the late 18th century, 13 American colonies broke free of British rule.
c. Four planes were hijacked in the United States on September 11, 2001.
d. In 2003, a dinosaur with feathers and four wings was found in China.
e. Since the late 1970s, HIV has infected more than 60 million people.
f. In 2008, Barack Obama beat John McCain to become U.S. president.
g. U.S. president John F. Kennedy was shot to death in 1963.
h. In 1953, Sir Edmund Hillary and the Sherpa Tenzing Norgay were the first to reach the summit of Mount Everest.

**B** PAIR WORK Give another example for each kind of historic event in part A.

"The exploration of Mars is an amazing achievement."

## 6 DISCUSSION It made a difference.

GROUP WORK Choose two or three historic events (an election, an epidemic, an achievement, etc.) that had an impact on your country. Discuss the questions.

What happened (or what was achieved)? When did it happen?
What was the immediate effect on your country? the world? your family?
Did it change things permanently? How is life different now?

"Recently a large oil field was discovered off the coast of Brazil. . . ."

## 7 WRITING A biography

**A** Find information about a person who has had a major influence on the world or your country. Answer these questions. Then write a biography.

What is this person famous for?
How and when did he or she become famous?
What are his or her important achievements?

**B** PAIR WORK Exchange biographies. What additional details can your partner add?

### Kim Dae-jung (1925–2009)

Kim Dae-jung became famous during the 1960s, when he was first elected to government. He became an opposition leader and spent many years in the 1970s and 1980s in prison.

He was president of South Korea from 1998 to 2003. He was awarded the Nobel Peace Prize in 2000 for his efforts toward peace, democracy, and human rights. Kim Dae-jung died . . .

## 8 INTERCHANGE 10 History buff

Find out how good you are at history.
Student A, go to Interchange 10A on page 124; Student B, go to Interchange 10B on page 126.

## 9 PERSPECTIVES

**A** ▶ Listen to a survey about the future. Check (✓) the predictions you think will happen.

# What will the future hold?

☐ Computers will recognize any voice command.
You won't need a keyboard.

☐ Within 20 years, scientists will have discovered
a cure for baldness.

☐ People will be living in cities under the ocean.

☐ By 2025, world leaders will have eliminated terrorism.

☐ Robots will be performing most factory jobs.

☐ By 2050, we will have set up human communities on Mars.

☐ Medical scientists will find a cure for Alzheimer's disease.

**B** Which of the predictions do you think will affect you?

## 10 GRAMMAR FOCUS

> ### Predicting the future with will ▶
>
> **Use will to predict future events or situations.**
> Computers **will recognize** any voice command. You **won't need** a keyboard.
>
> **Use future continuous to predict ongoing actions.**
> People **will be living** in cities under the ocean.
>
> **Use future perfect to predict actions that will be completed by a certain time.**
> Within 20 years, scientists **will have discovered** a cure for baldness.
> By 2050, we **will have set up** human communities on Mars.

**A** Complete these predictions with the correct verb forms. (More than one answer is possible.) Then compare with a partner.

1. In ten years, flights from New York to Tokyo ....................
   (take) less than two hours.
2. Soon, they .................... (sell) computers that can translate
   perfectly from one language to another.
3. By the middle of the twenty-first century, scientists
   .................... (discover) a way to prevent aging.
4. Sometime in the future, scientists .................... (invent) a
   machine that transmits our thoughts.
5. In the future, people .................... (live) on the moon.
6. In less than a decade, the polar ice caps .................... (melt),
   and many islands .................... (disappear).

**B** GROUP WORK  Discuss each prediction in part A. Do you agree or disagree?

A: In ten years, flights from New York to Tokyo will take less than two hours. What do you think?

B: Oh, I totally agree. I think they'll use space-shuttle technology to build faster airplanes.

C: I'm not so sure. Those flights normally take about 14 hours. How are they going to come up with an invention that shortens the trip by 12 hours?

**C** CLASS ACTIVITY  Discuss these questions.

1. What three recently developed technologies will have the greatest impact on our lives in the next 20 years?
2. What are the three most important changes that will have occurred on earth by 2050?
3. Which three jobs will people *not* be doing in 50 years? Why?

## 11 LISTENING  *A perfect future?*

**A** ▶ Listen to people discuss changes that will affect these topics of interest in the future. Write down two changes for each topic.

| Future changes | | |
| --- | --- | --- |
| 1. work | ............................................... | ............................................... |
| 2. transportation | ............................................... | ............................................... |
| 3. education | ............................................... | ............................................... |
| 4. health | ............................................... | ............................................... |

**B** GROUP WORK  Can you suggest one more possible change for each topic?

## 12 DISCUSSION  *Things will be different!*

GROUP WORK  Talk about these questions.

What do you think you'll be doing a year from now? five years from now?

Do you think you'll still be living in the same place?

What are three things you think you'll have accomplished within the next five years?

What are three things you won't have done within the next five years?

In what ways do you think you'll have changed by the time you retire?

# Food Trends National.com

HOME | **FOOD TRUCKS** | RESTAURANTS | FAST FOOD | CATERERS

# Tweet to eat

Chef Roy Choi
of Kogi BBQ

**Skim the article. What's innovative about Kogi BBQ's business model?**

As technology evolves, new business models emerge. For many years, businesses have sold their products and services online, but now social networking is changing the way people do business. Kogi BBQ in Los Angeles has found profitable ways to make the most of today's technology.

Kogi BBQ is a restaurant that serves a fusion of Korean and Mexican food concocted by Chef Roy Choi. The kimchi quesadilla and short rib taco are two favorites. Besides its menu, Kogi BBQ is different from other restaurants because people don't come to it; it goes to the people. Kogi BBQ uses five food-service trucks called Azul, Verde, Roja, Naranja, and Rosita to deliver cheap, gourmet fast food to long lines of hungry – and mostly young – customers throughout the city.

But how do people know where to find a Kogi BBQ truck? Technology is at the center of its business. Kogi BBQ uses the social networking site Twitter to inform customers where each of its trucks will be and when. The tweets (Twitter messages) look like this one:

> **Dinner time: Azul 6 PM - 9 PM @ Northridge (Devonshire and Reseda);**
> **10:30 PM - 11:30 PM @ City of Industry (18558 Gale Ave.)**

Customers can even post requests, like this one:

> **Can you come to Colima in Rowland Heights earlier? Maybe around 6-9? Thanks.**

Kogi BBQ has been a viral sensation in Los Angeles. In addition to Twitter, Kogi BBQ uses YouTube, Facebook, blogs, and other electronic tools, like text messaging, to stay connected with its customers. By avoiding traditional advertising and building its business around an online community, Kogi BBQ has created a "Kogi Kulture," fueled by dedicated fans eager to spread the word.

Time will tell if this is a passing fad or the wave of the future. Either way, this much is true: As technology changes, businesses will figure out how to capitalize on it.

**A** Read the article. Then complete the summary with information from the article.

........................... impacts the way people do ........................... . Kogi BBQ, a trendy restaurant in Los Angeles, has developed a successful business ........................... based on new technology. Kogi BBQ delivers gourmet fast food from five ........................... . To inform customers of their whereabouts, Kogi BBQ uses ........................... sites, like Twitter. In so doing, Kogi BBQ has built an online ........................... of enthusiastic customers who love and seek out its food.

**B** Use information in the article to answer the following questions in your own words.

1. Where does Kogi BBQ do business?
2. Why is Kogi BBQ considered fusion cuisine?
3. What is unique about Kogi BBQ?
4. What is a tweet?
5. What is "Kogi Kulture"?
6. What does it mean to *capitalize on* something?

**C** **GROUP WORK** What other companies use social networking to enhance their business? How might technology change the way people do business in the future?

# Units 9–10 Progress check

## SELF-ASSESSMENT

How well can you do these things? Check (✓) the boxes.

| I can . . . . | Very well | OK | A little |
|---|---|---|---|
| Describe experiences of getting/having things done (Ex. 1) | ☐ | ☐ | ☐ |
| Ask for and give advice about problems (Ex. 2) | ☐ | ☐ | ☐ |
| Understand and give descriptions of historical events (Ex. 3) | ☐ | ☐ | ☐ |
| Make predictions about the future (Ex. 4) | ☐ | ☐ | ☐ |

 **DISCUSSION** *Once in a while*

**GROUP WORK** Take turns asking questions about these services. When someone answers "yes,"
find out why and when the service was performed, and who performed it.

have your photo taken professionally
get your apartment painted
get your eyes checked
have your home redecorated or remodeled
get something translated

A: Have any of you ever had your photo taken professionally?
B: Yes, I have. I had one taken a few months ago.
C: Really? Why did you have it taken? . . .

**have a photo taken**

**2 ROLE PLAY** *A friend in need*

*Student A:* Choose one of these problems. Decide on the details of the
problem. Then tell your partner about it and get some advice.

I'm looking forward to my vacation, but I haven't saved enough money.
I don't get along with my . . . . We're always fighting.
I can't take care of my pet anymore. I don't know what to do.

*Student B:* Your partner tells you about a problem. Ask
questions about it. Then consider the situation
and offer two pieces of advice.

Change roles and choose another situation.

| useful expressions |
|---|
| Have you thought about . . .? |
| It might be a good idea to . . . |
| Maybe you could . . . |
| Why don't you . . . ? |

## 3  LISTENING  *How good is your history?*

**A**  Listen to people discuss the questions. Write the correct answers.

1. When was the first Iditarod? ............................................
2. How long did apartheid exist in South Africa? ............................................
3. When did a spacecraft first land on Mars? ............................................
4. How long was the Berlin Wall up? ............................................
5. How long have the modern Olympics existed? ............................................

**B GROUP WORK** Write three more questions about historic events. (Make sure you know the answers.) Then take turns asking your questions. Who has the most correct answers?

## 4  SURVEY  *Five years from now, . . .*

**A CLASS ACTIVITY** How many of your classmates will have done these things in the next five years? Write down the number of "yes" and "no" answers. When someone answers "yes," ask follow-up questions.

|  | "Yes" answers | "No" answers |
|---|---|---|
| 1. move to a new city | .................. | .................. |
| 2. get a (new) job | .................. | .................. |
| 3. have a(nother) child | .................. | .................. |
| 4. travel abroad | .................. | .................. |
| 5. learn another language | .................. | .................. |
| 6. get a college or master's degree | .................. | .................. |

A: Five years from now, will you have moved to a new city?
B: Yes, I think I will have moved away from here.
A: Where do you think you'll move to?
B: I'd like to live in Shanghai.
A: Really? What will you be doing there?

**B GROUP WORK** Tally the results of the survey as a group. Then take turns telling the class any additional information you found out.

"Very few people think they will have moved to a new city in five years. Only two people think that they will move. One person thinks he'll move to Shanghai, and one person thinks she'll move to Boston."

Shanghai

## WHAT'S NEXT

Look at your Self-assessment again. Do you need to review anything?

# 11 Life's little lessons

## 1 SNAPSHOT

### Rites of Passage
#### Some important life events

- First birthday (or first 100 days, as in South Korea)
- First haircut
- Losing your first tooth
- First day of school
- Sweet 16 (or Sweet 15, as in Latin America)
- First job
- High school graduation
- 20th birthday (or 21st birthday, as in the United States and Canada)
- College graduation
- Marriage
- Becoming a parent
- Retirement

Source: *Peace Corps Handbook for RPCV Speakers*

Which rites of passage, or life events, are important in your country?
   Check (✓) the events.
What are other rites of passage for people in your country?
Have any of these things recently happened to you or someone you know?

## 2 CONVERSATION  *I was really immature.*

**A** ▶ Listen and practice.

Alan: So what were you like when you were younger?
Carol: When I was a kid, I was kind of irresponsible.
Alan: You? Really? What made you change?
Carol: Graduating from high school.
Alan: What do you mean?
Carol: Well, until I graduated, I'd never had any important responsibilities. But then, I went off to college. . . .
Alan: I know what you mean. I was really immature when I was a teenager.
Carol: So what made *you* change?
Alan: I think I became more mature after I got my first job and moved away from home. Once I had a job, I became totally independent.
Carol: Where did you work?
Alan: I worked for my dad at the bank.

**B** ▶ Listen to the rest of the conversation.
What was another turning point for Carol? for Alan?

## Time clauses ▸

**Before** I had my first job, I was really immature.
**After** I got my first job, I became more mature.
**Once** I had a job, I became totally independent.
**The moment** I moved away from home, I felt like a different person.
**As soon as** I got my own bank account, I started to be more responsible.
**Until** I graduated, I'd never had any important responsibilities.
**By the time** I graduated from high school, I had already started working.

**A** Match the clauses in column A with appropriate information in column B.
Then compare with a partner.

**A**

1. By the time I was 15, ...........
2. Until I started working part-time, ...........
3. The moment I got my first paycheck, ...........
4. As soon as I left home, ...........
5. Once I started sharing an apartment, ...........
6. After I began a relationship, ...........
7. Before I traveled abroad, ...........
8. Until I got really sick, ...........

**B**

a. I didn't appreciate my own country.
b. I began to understand the value of money.
c. I learned that love can hurt!
d. I realized that I wasn't a child anymore.
e. I had learned how to take care of myself.
f. I learned how to get along better with people.
g. I had never saved any money.
h. I hadn't understood the importance of good health.

**B** Which of the clauses in column A can you relate to your life?
Add your own information to those clauses. Then compare with a partner.

"The moment I got my first paycheck, I became more independent."

**C** **GROUP WORK** What do you think people learn from these events? Write sentences
using time clauses in the present. Then take turns reading and talking about them.

1. getting a credit card
2. going out on your first date
3. getting your first job
4. getting your driver's license
5. buying your first bike, moped, or car
6. opening your own bank account
7. getting married
8. becoming a parent

> 1. Once you get a credit card, you learn
> it's important not to overspend.

## 4 LISTENING Important events

**A** ▶ Listen to three people describe important events in their lives. Complete the chart.

| | Event | How it affected him or her |
|---|---|---|
| **1.** Sally | ............................... | ............................... |
| **2.** Henry | ............................... | ............................... |
| **3.** Debbie | ............................... | ............................... |

**B** ▶ Listen again. What do these three people have in common?

## 5 SPEAKING Milestones

**A** **PAIR WORK** In your country, how old are people when these things happen?

get a driver's license  graduate from college
begin to date  get married
move out of their parents' home  retire

**B** **GROUP WORK** Choose three milestones. What do you think life is like before and after each one? Join another pair and discuss.

"Before people get a driver's license, they are very dependent on their parents. Once they get a license, they . . . "

## 6 WORD POWER Behavior and personality

**A** **PAIR WORK** At what age do you think people possess these traits? Check (✓) one or more ages for each trait.

| | In their teens | In their 20s | In their 30s | In their 40s | In their 60s |
|---|---|---|---|---|---|
| ambitious | ☐ | ☐ | ☐ | ☐ | ☐ |
| argumentative | ☐ | ☐ | ☐ | ☐ | ☐ |
| carefree | ☐ | ☐ | ☐ | ☐ | ☐ |
| conscientious | ☐ | ☐ | ☐ | ☐ | ☐ |
| naive | ☐ | ☐ | ☐ | ☐ | ☐ |
| pragmatic | ☐ | ☐ | ☐ | ☐ | ☐ |
| rebellious | ☐ | ☐ | ☐ | ☐ | ☐ |
| sensible | ☐ | ☐ | ☐ | ☐ | ☐ |
| sophisticated | ☐ | ☐ | ☐ | ☐ | ☐ |

**B** **GROUP WORK** Use the words in part A to describe people you know.

"My older brother is argumentative. He disagrees with me about everything!"

## 7 PERSPECTIVES  *I should have . . .*

**A** ▶ Listen to Maya Misery talk about her regrets. Do you have any similar regrets?

"I should have studied something more practical while I was in college."

"If I'd listened to my mother, I would have learned to play a musical instrument."

"If I'd been more ambitious in college, I could have learned to speak another language."

"I shouldn't have waited so long to choose a major."

"If I hadn't wasted so much money last year, I would have moved into my own apartment by now."

"If I hadn't been so irresponsible, I could have gotten better grades."

**B** What do you suggest to help Maya feel better?

## 8 GRAMMAR FOCUS

### Expressing regret and describing hypothetical situations ▶

**Use should have + the past participle to express regret.**
**I should have studied** something more practical when I was in college.
**I shouldn't have waited** so long to choose a major.

**Use would have + the past participle to express probable outcomes in hypothetical situations.**
**Use could have + the past participle to express possible outcomes.**
**If I**'**d listened** to my mother, I **would have learned** to play a musical instrument.
**If I hadn't been** so irresponsible, I **could have gotten** better grades.

**A** For each statement, write a sentence expressing regret. Then talk with a partner about which statements are true for you.

1. I was very rebellious when I was younger.
2. I didn't pay attention to what I ate as a kid.
3. I didn't make many friends in high school.
4. I was very argumentative as a teenager.
5. I was too naive when I started looking for my first job.

> 1. I should have been less rebellious when I was younger.

**B** Match the clauses in column A with appropriate information in column B.

**A**
1. If I'd listened to my parents, ...........
2. If I'd been more active, ...........
3. If I'd been more ambitious, ...........
4. If I'd studied harder in school, ...........
5. If I'd saved my money, ...........

**B**
a. I wouldn't have had to borrow so much.
b. I could have learned a lot more.
c. I would have made more pragmatic decisions.
d. I wouldn't have gained all this weight.
e. I could have gotten a promotion.

**C** Add your own information to the clauses in column A. Then compare in groups.

## 9 INTERCHANGE 11 *When I was younger, ...*

Imagine if things were different. Go to Interchange 11 on page 125.

## 10 PRONUNCIATION *Reduction of have and been*

**A** ▶ Listen and practice. Notice how **have** and **been** are reduced in these sentences.

I should **have been** less selfish when I was younger.
If I'd **been** more ambitious, I could **have** gotten a promotion.

**B** **PAIR WORK** Complete these sentences and practice them. Pay attention to the reduced forms of **have** and **been**.

I should have been . . . when I was younger.     If I'd been more . . . , I could have . . .
I should have been . . . in high school.          If I'd been less . . . , I would have . . .

## 11 LISTENING *Regrets*

**A** ▶ Listen to people describe their regrets. What does each person regret?

|  | What does he or she regret? | Why does he or she regret it? |
|---|---|---|
| **1.** Alex | ............................................... | ............................................... |
| **2.** Yi-yun | ............................................... | ............................................... |
| **3.** Jacob | ............................................... | ............................................... |

**B** ▶ Listen again. Why does he or she regret it?

## 12 WRITING *A letter of apology*

**A** Think about something you regret doing that you want to apologize for. Consider the questions below. Then write a letter of apology.

What did you do? What were the consequences?
Is there any way you can undo those consequences?

Dear Jonathan,
      I'm really sorry I forgot to tell you that my party was canceled. You worked so hard making all those cookies! I should've called or sent you a text before you started baking them, but I got really busy at work and didn't get around to it. If I'd been more conscientious, . . .

**B** **PAIR WORK** Read your partner's letter. Talk about what you would have done if you'd had a similar regret.

# 13 READING

## Milestones Around the World

_Scan the article. Where does each milestone take place? Who is each milestone for?_

### EGYPT

In Egypt, many families with new babies celebrate *El Sebou'*, which means *the seventh*. Some say the ancient pharaohs believed that children who lived to be seven days old were ready for a long and healthy life. Family and friends meet at the parents' house, and the baby is put in a round wooden cradle called a *ghorbal*. Songs are sung, and the baby is rocked gently to awaken its senses. Salt is scattered to keep evil away, and the mother carries the baby around the house. Children follow with lit candles. Finally, bags full of candies, sweets, and gold- and silver-like coins are distributed to all attendees.

### MEXICO

Families in Mexico and several other Latin American countries have a special celebration for *La quinceañera*, the birthday girl who turns 15 years old. It marks a girl's passage from girlhood to womanhood. Wearing a spectacular dress and carrying a bouquet of flowers, the girl arrives at a church for a thanksgiving service. Then there is a party with live music, dancing, and plenty of delicious food. An important moment is when the girl cuts a multilayered birthday cake.

### VANUATU

On a single island in the South Pacific nation of Vanuatu, young men hurl themselves from a 30-meter wooden tower, with only vines tied around their ankles to break their fall. The original bungee jumpers, these "land divers" jump to prove their manhood. The goal is for the young man's shoulder to just touch the ground. The vines' measurement must be exact as there is no safety net. When a young man jumps, his mother holds a favorite childhood item. After the jump, she throws the item away, demonstrating that he is now a man.

**A** Read the article. Find the words in *italics* in the article. Then match each word with its meaning.

........... 1. *senses*
........... 2. *scattered*
........... 3. *spectacular*
........... 4. *plenty*
........... 5. *hurl*
........... 6. *prove*

a. thrown in different directions
b. demonstrate
c. throw
d. sight, hearing, taste, touch, and smell
e. very exciting to look at
f. more than enough

**B** Check (✓) the correct milestone(s) for each description.

|  | El Sebou' | La quinceañera | Land diving |
|---|---|---|---|
| 1. The person's family participates. | ☐ | ☐ | ☐ |
| 2. There is a religious ceremony. | ☐ | ☐ | ☐ |
| 3. Children carry candles. | ☐ | ☐ | ☐ |
| 4. The event is dangerous. | ☐ | ☐ | ☐ |
| 5. The event requires special clothing. | ☐ | ☐ | ☐ |

**C GROUP WORK** Which of the milestones do you think is the most serious? Which is the most fun? Why do you think people celebrate milestones like these?

_Life's little lessons_ ■ 77

# The right stuff

## 1 SNAPSHOT

SUCCESS STORIES

Five of the world's most successful businesses

| COMPANY | MAIN PRODUCTS | FACT |
|---|---|---|
| Coca-Cola | soft drinks, juice, and bottled water | Coca-Cola is the best-known English word in the world after *OK*. |
| Sony | electronics equipment, movies, and TVs | Some early products included tape recorders and rice cookers. |
| Levi Strauss | jeans and casual clothing | The first jeans were made for men looking for gold in California. |
| Google | Internet-based products and services | Google comes from *googol*, which is the math term for the number 1 followed by 100 zeros. |
| Nestlé | chocolate, instant coffee, and bottled water | Nestlé means *little nest*, which symbolizes security and family. |

Sources: *Hoover's Handbook of American Business 2003*; www.sony.net; www.google.com; www.nestle.com

*Which of these products exist in your country? Are they successful?*
*Can you think of three successful companies in your country? What do they produce?*

## 2 PERSPECTIVES

**A** ▶ Listen to the survey. What makes a business successful?
Number the choices from 1 (most important) to 3 (least important).

**What makes a business successful?**

| 1 | Most important |
| 2 | Somewhat important |
| 3 | Least important |

1. In order for a language school to succeed, it has to have
   ☐ a variety of classes  ☐ a convenient location  ☐ inexpensive courses

2. To run a popular Internet café, it's a good idea to have
   ☐ plenty of computers  ☐ good snacks and drinks  ☐ a fast connection

3. In order to operate a successful movie theater, it has to have
   ☐ the latest movies  ☐ good snacks and drinks  ☐ big screens

4. To establish a trendy restaurant, it's important to have
   ☐ fashionable servers  ☐ delicious food  ☐ good music

5. For an athletic center to be profitable, it needs to have
   ☐ good trainers  ☐ modern exercise equipment  ☐ a variety of classes

6. For a concert hall to be successful, it should have
   ☐ excellent acoustics  ☐ comfortable seats  ☐ affordable tickets

**B** **GROUP WORK** Compare your answers. Do you agree on the most important success factors?

## PRONUNCIATION *Reduced words*

**A** ▶ Listen and practice. Notice how certain words are reduced in conversation.

In order **for a** café **to** succeed, it needs **to** have good food **and** service.
**For an** airline **to** be successful, it has **to** maintain **a** good safety record.

**B** **PAIR WORK** Take turns reading the sentences in Exercise 2 aloud. Use your first choice to complete each sentence. Pay attention to reduced words.

## GRAMMAR FOCUS

> ### Describing purpose ▶
>
> **Infinitive clauses**
>
> | **To run** a popular Internet café, | it's a good idea to have plenty of computers. |
> | **(In order) to establish** a trendy restaurant, | it's important to have fashionable servers. |
>
> **Infinitive clauses with for**
>
> | **For** an athletic center **to be** profitable, | it needs to have modern exercise equipment. |
> | **(In order) for** a language school **to succeed**, | it has to have a convenient location. |

**A** Match each goal with a suggestion. Then practice the sentences with a partner.

**Goals**

1. For a health club to attract new people, ............
2. In order to run a profitable restaurant, ............
3. To establish a successful dance club, ............
4. For a coffee bar to succeed, ............
5. To run a successful clothing boutique, ............

**Suggestions**

a. you need to hire a talented chef.
b. it's a good idea to offer desserts, too.
c. you need to keep up with the latest styles.
d. it needs to have great music and lighting.
e. it has to offer the latest equipment.

**B** **PAIR WORK** Give another suggestion for each goal in part A.

**C** **GROUP WORK** Look at the picture of a coffee shop. For it to stay in business, what should be done?

"For this coffee shop to stay in business, it needs . . ."

## 5 WORD POWER *Qualities for success*

**A PAIR WORK** What qualities are important for success?
Rank them from 1 to 5.

| A model | A salesperson | A magazine |
|---|---|---|
| ☐ fashionable | ☐ clever | ☐ affordable |
| ☐ gorgeous | ☐ charming | ☐ attractive |
| ☐ industrious | ☐ knowledgeable | ☐ entertaining |
| ☐ muscular | ☐ persuasive | ☐ informative |
| ☐ slender | ☐ tough | ☐ well written |

**B GROUP WORK** Add one more adjective to each list.

"For a model to be successful, he or she needs to be . . ."

## 6 ROLE PLAY *You're hired!*

*Student A:* Interview two people for one of these jobs. What qualities do they need for success? Decide who is more qualified for the job.

*Students B and C:* You are applying for the same job. What are your best qualities? Convince the interviewer that you are more qualified for the job.

host for a political talk show    server at a trendy café    exercise equipment salesperson

A: To be a good host for a political talk show, you need to be knowledgeable. Are you?
B: Yes. I follow politics closely, and I'm also tough. I'm not afraid to ask hard questions.
C: I'm fascinated by politics, and I'm industrious, so I would do thorough research.

## 7 CONVERSATION *I thought you'd never ask!*

**A**  Listen and practice.

Mayumi: What's your favorite club, Ben?
Ben: The Soul Club. They have fabulous music, and it's never crowded, so it's easy to get in.
Mayumi: That's funny. There's always a long wait outside my favorite club. I like it because it's always packed.
Ben: Why do you think it's so popular?
Mayumi: Well, it just opened a few months ago, everything is brand-new and modern, and lots of fashionable people go there. It's called the Casablanca.
Ben: Oh, right! I hear the reason people go there is just to be seen.
Mayumi: Exactly! Do you want to go some night?
Ben: I thought you'd never ask!

**B CLASS ACTIVITY** What are some popular places in your city?
Do you ever go to any of these places? Why or why not?

### Giving reasons ▶

I like the Casablanca **because** it's always packed.
**Since** it's always so packed, there's a long wait outside the club.
It's popular **because of** the fashionable people.
The Soul Club is famous **for** its fantastic music.
**Due to** the crowds, the Casablanca is difficult to get in to.
**The reason (that/why)** people go there **is** just to be seen.

**A** Complete the paragraph with *because, since, because of, for, due to*, and *the reason*. Then compare with a partner. (More than one answer is possible.)

MTV is one of the most popular television networks in the world. People love MTV not only ........................ its music videos, but also ........................ its clever and diverse programming. ........................ it keeps its shows up-to-the-minute, young people watch MTV for the latest fads in music and fashion. MTV is also well known ........................ its music awards show. ........................ so many people watch it is to see all the fashionable guests. MTV even has reality shows. These shows are popular ........................ they appeal to young people. ........................ MTV's widespread popularity, many teenagers have become less industrious with their homework!

**B** What reason explains the success of each situation? (More than one answer is possible.) Compare ideas with a partner.

**Situation**

1. Nokia is a successful company ............
2. People love Levi's jeans ............
3. The BBC is well known ............
4. Huge supermarket chains are popular ............
5. People everywhere drink Coca-Cola ............
6. Apple products are famous ............
7. Nike is a popular brand of clothing ............
8. Many people like megastores ............

**Reason**

a. since prices are generally more affordable.
b. due to its ever-changing product line.
c. because they have always been fashionable.
d. for their innovative designs.
e. because of its informative programming.
f. for their big choice of products.
g. since it advertises worldwide.
h. because the advertising is clever and entertaining.

**C** **PAIR WORK** Suggest two more reasons for each success in part B.

A: Nokia is a successful company because its commercials are very clever.
B: I think another reason why they are successful is . . .

## 9 LISTENING Radio commercials

**A** ▶ Listen to radio commercials for three different businesses. What are two special features of each place?

| Maggie's | Sports Pro | Mexi-Grill |
|---|---|---|
| 1. ................................. | ................................. | ................................. |
| 2. ................................. | ................................. | ................................. |

**B** ▶ Listen again. Complete each slogan.

1. "If you don't ................. what you want in your ................. , come ................. ours!"
2. "We're here to ................. you have ................. !"
3. "You won't find a ................. , ................. meal – anywhere!"

## 10 INTERCHANGE 12 Catchy slogans

How well do you know the slogans companies use for their products?
Go to Interchange 12 on page 127.

## 11 DISCUSSION TV commericials

**GROUP WORK** Discuss these questions.

When you watch TV, do you pay attention to the commercials? Why or why not?
What commercials do you remember from the last time you watched TV?
What are some effective commercials you remember? What made them effective?
What is the funniest commercial you've ever seen? the dumbest? the most shocking?
Which celebrities have been in commercials? Has this affected your opinion of the product?
    Has it affected your opinion of the celebrity?
What differences are there between commercials today and commercials from the past?

## 12 WRITING A commercial

**A** Choose one of your favorite products. Read the questions and make notes about the best way to sell it. Then write a one-minute radio or TV commercial.

What's good or unique about the product?
Why would someone want to buy or use it?
Can you think of a clever name or slogan?

**B GROUP WORK** Take turns presenting your commercials. What is good about each one?
Can you give any suggestions to improve them?

> Are you looking for a high-quality TV that is also attractively designed? Buy a Star TV. Star is the most popular name in electronics because of its commitment to excellence and . . .

# The Wrong Stuff

**Look at the picture and the first sentence of the article. Why is market research important to companies that want to sell their products internationally?**

If a business wants to sell its product internationally, it had better do some market research first. This is a lesson that some large American corporations have learned the hard way.

### What's in a name?

Sometimes the problem is the name. When General Motors introduced its Chevy Nova into Latin America, it overlooked the fact that *No va* in Spanish means "It doesn't go." Sure enough, the Chevy Nova never went anywhere in Latin America.

### Translation problems

Sometimes it's the slogan that doesn't work. No company knows this better than Pepsi-Cola, with its "Come alive with Pepsi!" campaign. The campaign was so successful in the United States that Pepsi translated its slogan literally for its international campaign. As it turned out, the translations weren't quite right. Pepsi was pleading with Germans to "Come out of the grave" and telling the Chinese that "Pepsi brings your ancestors back from the grave."

### A picture's worth a thousand words

Other times, the problem involves packaging. A picture of a smiling, round-cheeked baby has helped sell countless jars of Gerber baby food. So when Gerber marketed its products in Africa, it kept the picture on the jar. What Gerber didn't realize was that in many African countries, the picture on the jar shows what the jar has in it.

### Twist of fate

Even cultural factors can be involved. The cosmetics company Revlon made a costly mistake when they launched a new perfume in Brazil. The perfume smelled like Camellia flowers. It overlooked the fact that Camellia flowers are associated with funerals in Brazil. Unsurprisingly, the perfume failed. The entire Revlon brand suffered as many felt the company disrespected the culture.

Here's a great new car. The Nova!

It doesn't run?

**A** Read the article. Then for each statement, check (✓) True, False, or Not given.

|  | True | False | Not given |
|---|---|---|---|
| 1. General Motors did a lot of research before naming the Chevy Nova. | ☐ | ☐ | ☐ |
| 2. The "Come alive with Pepsi!" campaign worked well in the U.S. | ☐ | ☐ | ☐ |
| 3. Pepsi still sold well in Germany and China. | ☐ | ☐ | ☐ |
| 4. Gerber changed its packaging after the problem in Africa. | ☐ | ☐ | ☐ |
| 5. The problem for Revlon was the name "Camellia." | ☐ | ☐ | ☐ |
| 6. Revlon no longer sells cosmetics in Brazil. | ☐ | ☐ | ☐ |

**B** Look at the marketing problems below. In each situation, was the problem related to the product's name (**N**) or slogan (**S**)?

............ 1. The Ford Fiera didn't sell well in Spain, where *fiera* means "ugly old woman."

............ 2. Braniff Airline's "Fly in leather" campaign was meant to promote its comfortable new seats. In Spanish, the company was telling passengers to "Fly with no clothes on."

**C** **GROUP WORK** Think of two products sold in your country: one that has sold well, and one that hasn't. Why did one sell well, but not the other? What changes could help the second product sell better?

# Units 11–12 Progress check

## SELF-ASSESSMENT

How well can you do these things? Check (✓) the boxes.

| I can . . . . | Very well | OK | A little |
|---|---|---|---|
| Describe important life events and their consequences (Ex. 1) | ☐ | ☐ | ☐ |
| Describe and explain regrets about the past (Ex. 2) | ☐ | ☐ | ☐ |
| Describe hypothetical situations in the past (Ex. 2) | ☐ | ☐ | ☐ |
| Understand and give reasons for success (Ex. 3, 4) | ☐ | ☐ | ☐ |
| Describe the purpose of actions (Ex. 4) | ☐ | ☐ | ☐ |

## 1 SPEAKING Lessons to live by

**A** What are two important events for each of these age groups? Complete the chart.

| Children | Teenagers | People in their 20s | People in their 40s |
|---|---|---|---|
| .......................... | .......................... | .......................... | .......................... |
| .......................... | .......................... | .......................... | .......................... |

**B** GROUP WORK Talk about the events. Why is each event important? What do people learn from each event?

A: Starting school is an important event for children.
B: Why is starting school an important milestone?
A: Once they start school, . . .

| useful expressions | |
|---|---|
| after | once |
| as soon as | before |
| the moment | until |
| by the time | |

## 2 GAME A chain of events

**A** Write three regrets you have about the past.

**B** GROUP WORK What if the situations were different? Take turns. One student expresses a regret. The next student adds a hypothetical result, and so on, for as long as you can.

A: I should have been more ambitious during college.
B: If you'd been more ambitious, you would have gone abroad.
C: If you'd gone abroad, you could have . . .

## 3 LISTENING *Success story*

**A** ▶ Listen to a business consultant discuss the factors necessary for a restaurant to be successful. Check (✓) the ones she says are important.

☐ advertising    ☐ concept    ☐ decor    ☐ food    ☐ location    ☐ name

**B** ▶ Listen again. In your own words, write the reason why each factor is important.

| Factor | Why is it important? |
|--------|----------------------|
| **1.** ................................................ | ................................................ |
| **2.** ................................................ | ................................................ |
| **3.** ................................................ | ................................................ |

## 4 DISCUSSION *The secrets of success*

**A** **PAIR WORK** Choose two businesses and discuss what they need to be successful. Then write three sentences describing the most important factors.

☐ a car wash        ☐ a gourmet supermarket    ☐ a juice bar
☐ a dance club      ☐ a high-rise hotel        ☐ a used clothing store

> 1. In order for a hotel to be successful, it has to be affordable.

**B** **GROUP WORK** Join another pair. Share your ideas. Do they agree?

A: We think in order for a hotel to be successful, it has to be affordable.
B: Really? But some of the most successful hotels are very expensive.

**C** **GROUP WORK** Now choose a popular business that you know about. What are the reasons for its success?

"I think W hotels are successful because the decor is so beautiful."

W Santiago

| useful expressions |
|---|
| It's successful because (of) . . .      It's become popular since . . . |
| It's popular due to . . .               It's famous for. . . |
| The reason it's successful is . . . |

## WHAT'S NEXT?

Look at your Self-assessment again. Do you need to review anything?

 # That's a possibility.

## 1 SNAPSHOT

# Pet Peeves
## Why is it that some people...?

- ◆ are noisy eaters
- ◆ always ask for favors
- ◆ constantly interrupt
- ◆ are late all the time
- ◆ read over my shoulder on the subway
- ◆ chat online while talking on the phone
- ◆ always want to get in the last word
- ◆ throw their garbage in the recycling bin
- ◆ don't cover their mouths when they cough
- ◆ make popping sounds when they chew gum

Source: Interviews with people between the ages of 16 and 45

*Which of the pet peeves do you have about people you know? Which one is the worst?*
*Underline a pet peeve you could be accused of. When and why are you guilty of it?*
*Are there any pet peeves in the list that don't annoy you?*

## 2 CONVERSATION *What happened?*

**A** ▶ Listen and practice.

**Jackie:** You asked Beth to be here around 7:00, didn't you?
**Bill:** Yes. What time is it now?
**Jackie:** It's almost 8:00. I wonder what happened.
**Bill:** Hmm. She might have forgotten the time. Why don't I call and see if she's on her way?

*A few minutes later*

**Bill:** I got her voice mail, so she must not have turned on her cell phone.
**Jackie:** I hope she didn't have a problem on the road. Her car could have broken down or something.
**Bill:** Of course she may have simply forgotten and done something else today.
**Jackie:** No, she couldn't have forgotten – I just talked to her about it yesterday. I guess we should start without her.

**B** ▶ Listen to the rest of the conversation. What happened?

## 3 PRONUNCIATION *Reduction in past modals*

**A** ▶ Listen and practice. Notice how **have** is reduced in these sentences.

He must **have** forgotten the date.  She might **have** had a problem on the road.

**B** ▶ Listen and practice. Notice that **not** is not contracted or reduced in these sentences.

He may **not** have remembered it.  She must **not** have caught her bus.

## 4 GRAMMAR FOCUS

> ### Past modals for degrees of certainty ▶
>
> **It's almost certain.**
> She **must have left** already.
> She **must not have turned on** her phone.
>
> **It's not possible.**
> She **couldn't have been** at home.
>
> **It's possible.**
> She **may/might have forgotten** the time.
> She **may/might not have remembered** the time.
> Her car **could have broken down**.

**A** Read each situation and choose the best explanation. Then practice with a partner.
(Pay attention to the reduced forms in past modals.)

**Situation**

1. Maura couldn't keep her eyes open. ............
2. Brian got a call and looked worried. ............
3. The teacher looks very happy today. ............
4. Jane is in a terrible mood today. ............
5. Jeff was fired from his job. ............
6. My cousin is broke again. ............

**Explanation**

a. He may have gotten a raise.
b. She must not have gotten enough sleep.
c. He might not have done his work on time.
d. She could have had a fight with her boyfriend.
e. She must have spent too much last month.
f. He couldn't have heard good news.

**B PAIR WORK** Suggest different explanations for each situation in part A.

## 5 LISTENING *Jumping to conclusions*

**A GROUP WORK** What do you think happened? Offer an explanation for each event.

**B** ▶ Listen to the explanations for the two events in part A and take notes.
What *did* happen? How similar were your explanations?

## 6 SPEAKING What's your explanation?

**A** **PAIR WORK** What do you think were the reasons for these events? Suggest two different explanations for each.

1. Two people were having dinner in a restaurant. One suddenly got up and ran out of the restaurant.
2. A woman living alone returned home and found the TV and radio turned on. They weren't on when she went out.
3. Two friends met again after not seeing each other for many years. One looked at the other and burst out laughing.

**B** **GROUP WORK** Each student thinks of two situations like the ones in part A. Others suggest explanations.

A: Last night, a wife handed her husband a large bag of money.
B: Well, she might have returned some money she'd taken from him.

## 7 INTERCHANGE 13 Photo plays

What's your best explanation for some unusual events? Go to Interchange 13 on page 128.

## 8 PERSPECTIVES She's driving me crazy!

**A**  Listen to three friends talking to one another on the phone. Check (✓) the response you think is best for each person's problem.

**Michi** | **Molly**

Hi Molly. Ramona's mad because she thinks I didn't ask her to go hiking with us. I sent her four emails, but she never responded!

☐ Well, you know Ramona never answers emails. You should have called her on the phone.

☐ Oh, forget it! I wouldn't have sent so many messages. If Ramona can't bother to check her email, she'll just miss out on things.

**Molly** | **Ramona**

Ramona, hi! I just got off the phone with Michi. She asked me for advice, but she never stops talking long enough to listen!

☐ You could have been more understanding. Michi must have been upset and just needed to talk.

☐ I would have asked Michi to be quiet for a minute. How can you give her advice if she doesn't give you a chance to talk?

**Ramona** | **Michi**

Michi, I can't believe that Molly still has my notes! I needed them for a test today. She never returns things!

☐ Molly shouldn't have kept your notes this long! But I wouldn't have lent them to her the week before a test.

☐ Oh, Molly may have just forgotten about them. I would have just borrowed someone else's notes.

**B** Do you talk about pet peeves with your friends? Do they give you advice?

## 9 GRAMMAR FOCUS

> ### Past modals for judgments and suggestions ▶
>
> **Judging past actions**
> You **should have called** her on the phone.
> She **shouldn't have kept** your notes this long.
>
> **Suggesting alternative past actions**
> You **could have been** more understanding.
> I **wouldn't have lent** them to her.

**A** Complete the conversations using past modals with the verbs given. Then practice with a partner.

1. A: I invited my boyfriend over to meet my parents, but he arrived wearing torn jeans. He looked so messy!
   B: Well, he ............................................. (dress) neatly.
   I ............................................. (ask) him to wear something nicer.

2. A: John borrowed my car and dented it. When he returned it, he didn't even say anything about it!
   B: He ............................................. (tell) you! Well, I ............................................. (not lend) it to him in the first place. He's a terrible driver.

3. A: I'm exhausted. Mary came over and stayed until 2:00 A.M.!
   B: She ............................................. (not stay) so late. You ............................................. (start) yawning. Maybe she would have gotten the hint!

4. A: Tom invited me to a play, but I ended up paying for us both!
   B: I ............................................. (not pay) for him. He ............................................. (not invite) you if he didn't have enough money.

**B** **PAIR WORK** Think of another suggestion or comment for each situation above.

## 10 WORD POWER Reactions

**A** Megan's boyfriend forgot her birthday. How does she react? Match each reaction with the best example.

| Reaction | Example |
|---|---|
| 1. an assumption ............ | a. "If you do it again, you'll have to find a new girlfriend." |
| 2. a criticism ............ | b. "I bet you were out with another woman!" |
| 3. a demand ............ | c. "You can be so inconsiderate." |
| 4. an excuse ............ | d. "You'll probably forget our anniversary, too!" |
| 5. a prediction ............ | e. "Now you have to take me out to dinner . . . twice." |
| 6. a suggestion ............ | f. "You must have wanted to break up with me." |
| 7. a suspicion ............ | g. "You know, you ought to buy me flowers." |
| 8. a warning ............ | h. "I know you've been busy lately. It just slipped your mind." |

**B** **GROUP WORK** Imagine that someone was late for class, or choose another situation. Give an example of each reaction in the list above.

## 11 LISTENING What should they have done?

**A** ▶ Listen to descriptions of three situations. What would have been the best thing to do in each situation? Check (✓) the best suggestion.

1. ☐ Dennis should have called a locksmith.
   ☐ He should have broken a window.
   ☐ He did the right thing.

2. ☐ Diana should have turned up her radio to keep out the noise.
   ☐ She should have called the neighbors to see what was happening.
   ☐ She did the right thing.

3. ☐ Simon should have kept the ring for himself.
   ☐ He should have taken the ring and called the police.
   ☐ He did the right thing.

**B PAIR WORK** What would you have done in each situation in part A?

## 12 DISCUSSION You could have . . .

**GROUP WORK** Read each situation. Say what you could have or should have done.

"I went to my neighbor's house for dinner last night. He had cooked all day, but the food was awful! I didn't want to hurt his feelings, so I ate it."

"My friend forgot to do her homework, so she asked if she could look at mine. I did mine, but I told her I hadn't."

"I didn't have any money to buy my cousin a birthday present, so I gave her something I had received previously as a gift. My brother told my cousin and now she's mad at me."

"My friend started dating this guy I don't really like. She asked what I thought of him, and I told her the truth."

A: You should have told him you weren't feeling well.
B: Or you could have eaten it really slowly.
C: I think I would have . . .

## 13 WRITING A complicated situation

**A** Think of a complicated situation from your own experience. Write a paragraph describing the situation, but don't explain how you resolved it.

One friend of mine is very demanding of my time. He wants to do everything with me, and I have a hard time saying no. I have other friends I want to spend time with as well. Last night, he asked me to spend all day Saturday with him. I didn't want to hurt his feelings. . . .

**B PAIR WORK** Exchange papers. Write a short paragraph about how you would have resolved your partner's situation.

**C PAIR WORK** Read your partner's resolution to your situation. Tell your partner how you resolved it. Whose resolution was better?

# The Blue Lights of Silver Cliff

**Look at the picture. What do you think the "blue lights" are?**

Today, the town of Silver Cliff, Colorado, has a population of only 100 people. Once, however, it was a prosperous mining town where thousands came with dreams of finding silver and making their fortune.

Late one night in 1880, a group of miners were headed back to their camp after a good time in town. They were still laughing and joking as they approached the graveyard on a hill outside Silver Cliff. Then one of the men yelled and pointed toward the graveyard. The others fell silent. On top of each grave, they saw flamelike blue lights. These eerie lights seemed to be dancing on the graves, disappearing and then appearing again.

This was the first sighting of the blue lights of Silver Cliff. There have been many other sightings over the years. In 1969, Edward Lineham from National Geographic magazine visited the graveyard. Lineham's article tells of his experience: "I saw them. . . . Dim, round spots of blue-white light glowed ethereally among the graves. I . . . stepped forward for a better look. They vanished. I aimed my flashlight at one eerie glow and switched it on. It revealed only a tombstone."

Lineham and others have suggested various explanations for the lights. The lights might have been reflections of lights from the town, but Silver Cliff's lights seemed too dim to have this effect. They could have been caused by radioactive ore, though there's no evidence of radioactivity. They may also have been caused by gases from rotting matter. This usually happens in swamps, however, and the area around Silver Cliff is dry. Or, perhaps, the lights are from the helmets of dead miners wandering the hills in search of their fortune.

**A** Read the article. Then answer these questions.

1. How has Silver Cliff changed over the years?
2. Where were the blue lights first seen?
3. Who saw the blue lights first?
4. What do the blue lights look like?

**B** Which of these statements are facts? Which are opinions? Check (✓) Fact or Opinion.

| | Fact | Opinion |
|---|---|---|
| **1.** Today, the town of Silver Cliff has a population of 100 people. | ☐ | ☐ |
| **2.** The miners saw flamelike blue lights on top of each grave. | ☐ | ☐ |
| **3.** Edward Lineham suggested various explanations for the lights. | ☐ | ☐ |
| **4.** The lights were actually reflections of lights from the town. | ☐ | ☐ |
| **5.** There was no evidence of radioactivity. | ☐ | ☐ |
| **6.** The lights were from the helmets of dead miners. | ☐ | ☐ |

**C** **GROUP WORK** Which of the explanations for the blue lights do you think is the most satisfactory? Why? Can you think of any other possible explanations?

# 14 Behind the scenes

**1** **SNAPSHOT**

## Movie Firms

**The first...**

- Movie-length music video – *Pink Floyd: The Wall* (1982)
- Advanced computer technology – *Terminator 2* (1991)
- Movie with Dolby Digital sound – *Batman Returns* (1992)
- Computer-animated feature film – *Toy Story* (1995)

- Movie to be released on DVD – *Twister* (1996)
- Movie to gross over $1 billion – *Titanic* (1998)
- 3-D movie to gross over $2 billion worldwide – *Avatar* (2009)
- Movie to make over $92 million in one day – *Harry Potter and the Deathly Hallows – Part 2* (2011)

Sources: www.imdb.com; www.listology.com

*Have you seen any of these movies? Did you enjoy them?*
*What's the most popular movie playing right now? Have you seen it? Do you plan to?*
*Are there many movies made in your country? Name a few of your favorites.*

**2** **CONVERSATION** *Movies are hard work!*

**A** ▶ Listen and practice.

Ryan: Working on movies must be really exciting.
Nina: Oh, yeah, but it's also very hard work.
A one-minute scene in a film can take days to shoot.
Ryan: Really? Why is that?
Nina: Well, a scene isn't filmed just once. Lots of different shots have to be taken. Only the best ones are used in the final film.
Ryan: So, how many times does a typical scene need to be shot?
Nina: It depends, but sometimes as many as 20 times. One scene may be shot from five or six different angles.
Ryan: Wow! I didn't realize that.
Nina: Why don't you come visit the studio? I can show you how things are done.
Ryan: Great, I'd love to!

**B** ▶ Listen to the rest of the conversation.
What else makes working on movies difficult?

## 3 GRAMMAR FOCUS

> **The passive to describe process** ⏵
>
> **is/are + past participle**
> A scene **isn't filmed** just once.
> Only the best shots **are used**.
>
> **Modal + be + past participle**
> One scene **may be shot** from five or six different angles.
> Lots of different shots **have to be taken**.

**A** The sentences below describe how a movie is made. First, complete the sentences using the passive. Then compare with a partner.

*Before filming*

☐ To complete the script, it has to ..................... (divide) into scenes, and the filming details need to ..................... (write out).

1 First, an outline of the script has to ..................... (prepare).

☐ Next, actors ..................... (choose), locations ..................... (pick), and costumes ..................... (design). Filming can then begin.

☐ Then the outline ..................... (expand) into a script.

☐ After the script ..................... (complete), a director must ..................... (hire).

*During and after filming*

☐ The final film you see on the screen ..................... (create) by the director and editor out of thousands of different shots.

☐ Soon after the film has been edited, music ..................... (compose) and sound effects may ..................... (add).

☐ After the filming ..................... (finish), the different shots can then ..................... (put together) by the editor and director.

6 Once shooting begins, different shots ..................... (film) separately. Scenes may ..................... (not shoot) in sequence.

**B** **PAIR WORK** Number the sentences in part A (before filming: from 1 to 5; during and after filming: from 6 to 9).

## 4 LISTENING *I love my job!*

**A** ⏵ Listen to an interview with a TV producer. Write down three things a producer does.

| Things a producer does | Personality traits |
| --- | --- |
| 1. ..................... | ..................... |
| 2. ..................... | ..................... |
| 3. ..................... | ..................... |

**B** ⏵ Listen again. What are three personality traits a producer should have? Complete the chart.

## 5 SPEAKING Step by step

**A** PAIR WORK What do you think is required to prepare for a theater performance? Put the pictures in order and describe the steps. Use the vocabulary to help you.

make the costumes

rehearse the lines

build the sets

choose the actors

find a venue

write the script

A: Preparing for a theater performance requires many steps.
First, the script must be written.
B: Right! And after that, the actors are chosen.
A: I agree. Then . . .

**B** PAIR WORK Choose one of these topics. Come up with as many steps as you can.

creating a student newspaper       planning a wedding              preparing for a rock concert
making a short video                preparing for a fashion show   putting on a school musical

**C** GROUP WORK Share your information from part B with another pair.

## 6 WRITING Describing a process

**A** Write about one of the topics from Exercise 5 or use your own idea. Describe the different steps in the process.

> Putting on a school musical requires a lot of planning.
> First, the director and production team must be chosen.
> Then the dates for the musical should be decided.
> After that, the actual musical can be chosen. Then
> auditions for the various roles can be held and . . .

**B** PAIR WORK Read your partner's paper. Can you think of any more steps?

## 7 WORD POWER  *Media professions*

**A** What kind of jobs are these? Complete the chart with the compound nouns.

| | | | |
|---|---|---|---|
| computer programmer | network installer | photo editor | software designer |
| editorial director | newscaster | movie extra | stunt person |
| film composer | page designer | sitcom writer | talk show host |

| Film jobs | Publishing jobs | TV jobs | Computer jobs |
|---|---|---|---|
| .................................... | .................................... | .................................... | .................................... |
| .................................... | .................................... | .................................... | .................................... |
| .................................... | .................................... | .................................... | .................................... |

**B** GROUP WORK  Choose four jobs from part A and describe what they do.

"A computer programmer writes the instructions that direct computers to process information."

## 8 PERSPECTIVES  *Quiz show*

**A** ▶ Listen to a quiz show. Can you guess the occupations?

| | |
|---|---|
| casting director | **1.** A _____, who finds appropriate places to shoot scenes, gets to travel all over the world. |
| location scout | **2.** A _____ is someone who chooses an actor for each part in a movie. |
| screenwriter | **3.** A _____, who makes sure that everything on a movie set looks realistic, creates the objects that the characters use. |
| dialect coach | **4.** A _____ is someone who develops and expands a story idea into a full movie script. |
| prop designer | **5.** A _____ is a language specialist who works with actors on their accents. |
| script doctor | **6.** A _____, who is used when an original screenplay needs more work, makes jokes funnier and dialogs more realistic. |

**B** Which of the jobs in part A do you think would be the most interesting? Why? Tell the class.

## 9 PRONUNCIATION  *Review of stress in compound nouns*

**A** ▶ Listen and practice. Notice how the first word in a compound noun usually receives greater stress.

newscaster     photo editor     movie extra     sitcom writer     stunt person

**B** Practice the sentences in Exercise 8. Pay attention to the word stress in the compound nouns.

### Defining and non-defining relative clauses ▶

**Defining relative clauses are used to identify people.**

A dialect coach is a language specialist.  ⟶  A dialect coach is a language specialist **who/that**
She works with actors on their accents.  **works with actors on their accents**.

**Non-defining relative clauses give further information about people.**

A location scout finds places to shoot  ⟶  A location scout, **who finds places to**
scenes. He travels all over the world.  **shoot scenes**, travels all over the world.

**A** Do these sentences contain defining (**D**) or non-defining (**ND**) clauses? Add commas to the non-defining clauses. Then compare with a partner.

1. A stunt person is someone who "stands in" for an actor during dangerous scenes. ............
2. A computer-graphics supervisor who needs advanced technical knowledge often spends millions of dollars on computer graphics. ............
3. A stagehand is the person who moves the sets on stage in a theater production. ............
4. A movie producer who controls the budget decides how money will be spent. ............

a stunt person

**B** Add the non-defining relative clauses in parentheses to the sentences.

1. A movie extra appears in the background scenes.
   (who never has any lines)

   ...................................................................................................
   ...................................................................................................

2. A newscaster presents the news and introduces videos from reporters.
   (who should be trustworthy)

   ...................................................................................................
   ...................................................................................................

3. A photo editor selects the photos that go into magazines.
   (who is responsible for the quality and content of images )

   ...................................................................................................
   ...................................................................................................

4. A film composer must know music theory and interpretation.
   (who writes the background music for movies)

   ...................................................................................................
   ...................................................................................................

**C** Write three sentences with relative clauses about jobs you know. Compare with a partner.

**11** *INTERCHANGE 14* *Who makes it happen?*

What kinds of people does it take to make a movie? Go to Interchange 14 on page 129.

# *Hooray for Bollywood!*

**Scan the article. Who do you think it was written for?**
■ people in the film industry   ■ the general public   ■ fans of Bollywood movies

**1** A storm forces a plane to make an emergency landing on a deserted island. The only shelter is a spooky house, where a murderer begins killing passengers. So what do these defenseless people do? They have a beach party and perform an elaborate song-and-dance number.

**2** This is the world of Bollywood. The scene described above is from the classic Indian film *Gumnaam*, which was made in the 1960s. It is typical of the kind of movies that are still made in India today.

**3** For as long as Hollywood has existed, there has also been an Indian film industry. Because it is based in Mumbai (formerly Bombay), it is popularly called Bollywood – from the words Bombay and Hollywood. While it is as old as Hollywood, it is much bigger. Bollywood currently has the largest movie industry in the world. It produces more than 1,100 films a year – and as many as 20 million people a day pack into movie theaters to see Bollywood films.

**4** While there are many types of films made in India, the most popular are the movies made in Bollywood. The films, which are made in the

Hindi language, generally deal with Indian history and social issues. The average Bollywood film runs about three hours but audiences don't seem to mind the length. The stories are melodramatic: Heroes drive around in flashy cars, actresses twirl around in beautiful costumes, and the poor boy always triumphs against the rich villain. They also feature many musical numbers, usually love songs.

**5** Although the films may seem exaggerated to some, that's not how most filmgoers feel. These movies and their stars are beloved by audiences throughout Asia, Africa, and the Middle East. "Every South Asian grows up with some kind of connection to Bollywood," notes Indian writer Suketu Mehta. "In certain ways, it's what unites us."

**A** Read the article. Find and underline a sentence in the article that answers each question below.

1. How does Bollywood compare to Hollywood?
2. How many Bollywood films are made every year?
3. How long is a typical Bollywood movie?
4. How do audiences feel about the stars of Bollywood movies?

**B** Find these sentences in the article. Decide whether each sentence is the main idea or a supporting idea in that paragraph. Check (✓) the correct boxes.

|  | Main idea | Supporting idea |
|---|---|---|
| 1. This is the world of Bollywood. (par. 2) | ☐ | ☐ |
| 2. It produces more than . . . to see Bollywood films. (par. 3) | ☐ | ☐ |
| 3. While there are many . . . made in Bollywood. (par. 4) | ☐ | ☐ |
| 4. The average Bollywood film . . . mind the length. (par. 4) | ☐ | ☐ |
| 5. Although the films may seem . . . filmgoers feel. (par. 5) | ☐ | ☐ |

**C** **GROUP WORK** Have you ever seen a Bollywood movie? If so, how did you like it?

# Units 13–14 Progress check

## SELF-ASSESSMENT

How well can you do these things? Check (✓) the boxes.

| I can . . . . | Very well | OK | A little |
|---|---|---|---|
| Understand and speculate about past events (Ex. 1) | ☐ | ☐ | ☐ |
| Make judgments and suggestions about past events (Ex. 2) | ☐ | ☐ | ☐ |
| Describe processes (Ex. 3) | ☐ | ☐ | ☐ |
| Describe people's appearance, personality, and typical behavior (Ex. 4) | ☐ | ☐ | ☐ |

## 1 LISTENING  *Where did it take place?*

**A** ▶ Listen to three conversations. Where do you think each conversation takes place? What do you think might have happened? Take notes.

| Where the conversation takes place | What might have happened |
|---|---|
| 1. ...................................................... | ...................................................... |
| 2. ...................................................... | ...................................................... |
| 3. ...................................................... | ...................................................... |

**B** **PAIR WORK** Compare your notes. Decide on what happened.

## 2 DISCUSSION  *Tricky situations*

**A** **PAIR WORK** React to these situations. First, make a judgment or suggestion using a past modal. Then add another statement using the reaction in parentheses.

1. John was driving too fast, and the police stopped him. (a warning)
2. Lisa got an F on her English test. (a criticism)
3. Bill went shopping and spent too much money. (an excuse)
4. Crystal is late to class every morning. (a suggestion)
5. Oscar studied all night for his final exam and didn't sleep at all. (a prediction)

"John shouldn't have driven so fast. He'd better be careful, or . . ."

**B** **GROUP WORK** Join another pair and compare your comments. Who has the most interesting reaction to each situation?

## GAME *From first to last*

**A** **GROUP WORK** Look at these topics. Set a time limit. Talk with your group and write as many steps as you can between the first and last parts of each process.

sending an email

making a cup of tea

First, the computer has to be turned on.

..................................................................
..................................................................
..................................................................
..................................................................
..................................................................

Finally, the email is delivered to the person's in-box.

First, some water must be boiled.

..................................................................
..................................................................
..................................................................
..................................................................
..................................................................

Finally, the tea has to be poured from the teapot into the cup.

**B** **CLASS ACTIVITY** Compare your answers. Which group has the most steps?

## SPEAKING *People in your life*

**A** Complete these statements about people in your life.

My mother is a person who ...................................... .
My neighbor, who ...................... , always ....................................... .
My father is a ...................... who ....................................... .
My teacher, who ...................... , is ....................................... .
My best friend is someone that ....................................... .

**B** **PAIR WORK** Compare your answers. Ask two follow-up questions about each of your partner's statements.

A: My mother is a person who takes care of everyone's needs before her own.
B: Does she ever get tired of helping everyone but herself?

## WHAT'S NEXT?

Look at your Self-assessment again. Do you need to review anything?

# 15 There should be a law!

1 **SNAPSHOT**

## It's Against the Law!

| In the United States and Canada | In other countries |
|---|---|

- In Arizona, you may go to prison for 25 years if you cut down a saguaro cactus.
- In New Britain, Connecticut, fire trucks must travel at 25 miles per hour even when going to a fire.
- In the state of Washington, it is illegal to pretend your parents are rich.
- In Canada, 35% of radio broadcasting time must have Canadian content.

**Police**

- In Switzerland, it's an offense to hang clothes out to dry on a Sunday.
- In Australia, it is illegal to walk on the right side of footpaths.
- It is against the law not to flush a public toilet in Singapore.
- In Finland, taxi drivers must pay royalties if they play music for customers.

Sources: www.dumblaws.com

*Which of these laws would you like to have in your city or country? Why?*
*Can you think of reasons for these laws?*
*Do you know of any other unusual laws?*

2 **PERSPECTIVES**

**A** ▶ Listen to people make recommendations at a community meeting. Would you agree with these proposals if they were made in your community? Check (✓) your opinion.

## Community Meeting Notes

|  | strongly agree | somewhat agree | disagree |
|---|---|---|---|
| 1. Cyclists should be required to wear helmets. | ☐ | ☐ | ☐ |
| 2. Pet owners shouldn't be allowed to walk dogs without a leash. | ☐ | ☐ | ☐ |
| 3. People ought to be required to end parties at midnight. | ☐ | ☐ | ☐ |
| 4. Something has got to be done to stop littering. | ☐ | ☐ | ☐ |
| 5. People mustn't be permitted to park motorcycles on the sidewalks. | ☐ | ☐ | ☐ |
| 6. Laws must be passed to control the noise from car alarms. | ☐ | ☐ | ☐ |
| 7. Drivers should only be permitted to honk their horns in case of an emergency. | ☐ | ☐ | ☐ |

**B GROUP WORK** Compare your opinions. If you have different opinions, give reasons for your opinions to try to get your classmates to agree with you.

# 3 GRAMMAR FOCUS

## Giving recommendations and opinions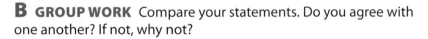

**When you think something is a good idea**
Cyclists **should be required** to wear a helmet.
Pet owners **shouldn't be allowed** to walk dogs without a leash.
People **ought (not) to be required** to end parties at midnight.

**When you think something is absolutely necessary**
Laws **must be passed** to control the noise from car alarms.
People **mustn't be permitted** to park motorcycles on the sidewalks.
A rule **has to be made** to require cycling lanes on city streets.
Something **has got to be done** to stop littering.

**A** Complete the sentences positively or negatively. Choose a modal that shows how strongly you feel about these issues.

1. People ........................... (allow) to use cell phones while driving.
2. Young people ........................... (permit) to get married before age 15.
3. Companies ........................... (require) to give workers periodic breaks.
4. People ........................... (allow) to have pets in high-rise apartments.
5. Scientists ........................... (permit) to use animals for research.
6. Laws ........................... (pass) to ban the sale of handguns.
7. The sale of fur products ........................... (prohibit).
8. Something ........................... (do) to stop clubs from staying open so late.

**B** **GROUP WORK** Compare your statements. Do you agree with one another? If not, why not?

A: People shouldn't be allowed to use cell phones while driving. It's dangerous.
B: You may have a point, but laws shouldn't be passed to prevent it. That's too strict.
C: Maybe, but in my opinion, . . .

# 4 DISCUSSION *What's your opinion?*

**A** **GROUP WORK** Think of three reasons for, and three reasons against, each idea below. Then discuss your views. As a group, form an opinion about each idea.

imposing strict dress codes for students
requiring people to do volunteer work
paying teachers less when their students fail

A: What do you think about imposing strict dress codes for students?
B: I think it's a terrible idea! Students shouldn't be required . . .

| offering a different opinion |
| --- |
| That sounds interesting, but I think . . . |
| That's not a bad idea. On the other hand, I feel . . . |
| You may have a point. However, I think . . . |

**B** **CLASS ACTIVITY** Share your group's opinions and reasons. Who has the most persuasive reasons for and against each position?

## 5 LISTENING *What should be done?*

**A** ▶ Listen to people discuss problems. What solutions do they suggest? Take notes in the chart.

1. people talking loudly on cell phones in restaurants
2. car alarms going off at night
3. telemarketing salespeople calling too often

| Solutions |
|---|
| 1. ................................................................................................................................ |
| 2. ................................................................................................................................ |
| 3. ................................................................................................................................ |

**B** **GROUP WORK** Do you agree or disagree with the solutions? What do you think should be done about each problem?

## 6 INTERCHANGE 15 *You be the judge!*

What if you could make the rules? Go to Interchange 15 on page 130.

## 7 WORD POWER *Local concerns*

**A** **PAIR WORK** Which of these issues are problems in your community? Check (✓) the appropriate boxes.

- ☐ bullying
- ☐ company outsourcing
- ☐ graffiti
- ☐ homelessness
- ☐ inadequate health care
- ☐ lack of affordable child care
- ☐ noise pollution
- ☐ overcrowded classrooms
- ☐ stray animals
- ☐ street crime

noise pollution

**B** **GROUP WORK** Join another pair of students. Which three problems concern your group the most? What should or can be done about them?

## 8 CONVERSATION  *It isn't cheap, is it?*

**A** ▶ Listen and practice.

Sarah: Health insurance, child-care bills, rent! Now that I'm going to school and only working part-time, I have a hard time making ends meet.

Todd: Health insurance is really expensive, isn't it?

Sarah: Yeah! My company used to pay for it when I was working full-time.

Todd: And child care isn't cheap, is it?

Sarah: No, it's not. After I pay for rent and groceries, almost all my money goes to pay for my son's day care.

Todd: Colleges should provide free day care for students with children.

Sarah: I think so, too. But they don't have any services like that at my school.

**B** ▶ Listen to the rest of the conversation. What is Todd concerned about?

## 9 GRAMMAR FOCUS

### Tag questions for opinions ▶

| **Affirmative statement + negative tag** | **Negative statement + affirmative tag** |
|---|---|
| Health insurance is really expensive, **isn't it**? | Child care isn't cheap, **is it**? |
| There are lots of criminals in the city, **aren't there**? | There aren't enough police, **are there**? |
| Graffiti makes everything look ugly, **doesn't it**? | People don't care about our city, **do they**? |
| Colleges should provide day care, **shouldn't they**? | You can't find affordable child care, **can you**? |

**A** Add tag questions to these statements. Then compare with a partner.

1. You can't escape advertising nowadays, . . . ?
2. There aren't any noise pollution laws, . . . ?
3. School bullying is a major problem here, . . . ?
4. Overcrowded classrooms can be hard to manage, . . . ?
5. The sales tax should be lowered, . . . ?
6. It isn't easy to save money these days, . . . ?
7. The city doesn't do enough for stray animals, . . . ?
8. There are more homeless people on the streets, . . . ?

**B** What are some things you feel strongly about in your school or city? Write six statements with tag questions.

**C** GROUP WORK Take turns reading your statements. Other students respond by giving their opinions.

A: The food in the cafeteria is terrible, isn't it?
B: Yes, it is. They should get a new cook.
C: On the other hand, I like the hamburgers because . . .

## 10 PRONUNCIATION  *Intonation in tag questions*

**A** ◉ Listen and practice. Use falling intonation in tag questions when you are giving an opinion and expect the other person to agree.

Street crime is a terrible problem, isn't it?

People should have access to quality health care, shouldn't they?

**B** **PAIR WORK** Take turns reading the statements with tag questions from Exercise 9, part A. Give your own opinions when responding.

## 11 LISTENING  *You agree, don't you?*

**A** ◉ Listen to people give their opinions about current issues in the news. What issues are they talking about?

| Issue | Opinions for | Opinions against |
|---|---|---|
| 1. .................................. | .................................. | .................................. |
|  | .................................. | .................................. |
| 2. .................................. | .................................. | .................................. |
|  | .................................. | .................................. |

**B** ◉ Listen again. What opinions do you hear? Complete the chart.

**C** **GROUP WORK** What do you think about the issues in part A?

## 12 WRITING  *A new law*

**A** Think about a local problem that needs to be solved, and write a persuasive essay suggesting a new law to help solve it. Be creative! Use these questions to help you.

What is the problem, and how does it affect your community?
What can be done to help solve it?
Who might disagree with you, and how will you convince them
    that your law is a good idea?

> I think students in our town should be required to wear school uniforms. Students shouldn't be permitted to wear the latest fashions because this promotes jealousy and competition. Also, students would be able to concentrate on their studies better if . . .

**B** **GROUP WORK** Try to convince your classmates to pass your new law. Then vote on it.

# How Serious Is Plagiarism?

**Read the title and first paragraph of the article. What do you think the word plagiarism means?**

In 2002, a biology teacher in Kansas – a state in the American Midwest – made national, and even international, news. After Christine Pelton discovered that 28 of her 118 students had plagiarized parts of a major project, she gave them failing grades. Although this was the school policy, the students' parents complained. The school board directed Ms. Pelton to change the punishment: They told her that 600 points should be taken from the offenders, rather than the entire 1,800 points. Ms. Pelton resigned in protest.

Why did this become such a significant story? Perhaps it is because so many people feel strongly about what is right and wrong. The incident raised some important questions: What is plagiarism? How serious is it?

The simplest form of plagiarism occurs when someone copies material without giving credit to the source. However, there are also more serious forms, such as when a student pays someone else to write an essay.

Some people claim that copying is necessary to do well in school. They have realized that their own words are not as good as someone else's. Another common argument is that everyone does it, so it's not a big deal. In fact, it has been learned that even some highly respected figures, including Martin Luther King Jr., have plagiarized.

Although some people find reasons to justify plagiarism, others feel the issue is clear-cut: They feel it is morally wrong, and consider it stealing – a theft of ideas rather than money. These people believe that students who plagiarize benefit unfairly. They receive a better grade than they deserve.

So what about the incident in Kansas? Was the original punishment too severe? Do teachers have the right to tell students and parents what is right or wrong? Ms. Pelton would probably say that the job of a teacher is to do exactly that.

**A** Read the article. Then number these sentences from 1 (first event) to 6 (last event).

............ a. The teacher's story appeared in national news.
............ b. The teacher gave the students failing grades.
............ c. The students' parents were angry.
............ d. The teacher left her job.
............ e. The group of students cheated on an assignment.
............ f. The school board told the teacher to change the scores.

**B** Complete the chart with the arguments for and against plagiarism presented in the article.

| Arguments to justify plagiarism | Arguments against plagiarism |
|---|---|
| 1. ................................................................ | ................................................................ |
| 2. ................................................................ | ................................................................ |

**C** **GROUP WORK** Is it ever OK to copy other people's work? Why or why not?
Should teachers have the right to tell students and parents what is right or wrong?

# 16 Challenges and accomplishments

## 1 SNAPSHOT

**VOLUNTEER!** What are you interested in? Consider these volunteering opportunities.

### COSTA RICA
- helping at a wildlife center
- monitoring endangered birds
- assisting with reforestation
- teaching computer skills
- organizing environmental activities

### THAILAND
- repairing rural roads
- building schools
- designing websites
- taking care of elephants
- working in rural health clinics

### MOZAMBIQUE
- building houses
- working at an orphanage
- conducting health surveys
- teaching English
- working on a marine conservation project

Sources: www.volunteerabroad.com; www.kayavolunteer.com

Which project sounds the most interesting? the least interesting?
Can you think of any other interesting projects that volunteers could do?
Do you know anyone who has volunteered? What did they do?

## 2 PERSPECTIVES *Volunteers talk about their work.*

**A** ▶ Listen to people talk about their volunteer work. What kind of work do they do? Write the names in the sentences below.

> The most rewarding thing about helping them is learning from their years of experience.
> —Paul

> One of the most difficult aspects of working abroad is being away from my family.
> —Sho-fang

> One of the rewards of working with them is experiencing their youthful energy and playfulness.
> —Mariela

> The most challenging thing about doing this type of work is determining their strengths and weaknesses.
> —Jack

1. .................... teaches in a developing country.
2. .................... tutors in an adult literacy program.
3. .................... visits senior citizens in a nursing home.
4. .................... plays games with children in an orphanage.

**B** Which kind of volunteer work would you prefer to do? What do you think would be rewarding or challenging about it?

## 3 GRAMMAR FOCUS

> ### Complex noun phrases containing gerunds ▶
>
> **The most rewarding thing about helping them** is learning from their years of experience.
> **One of the most difficult aspects of working abroad** is being away from my family.
> **One of the rewards of working with them** is experiencing their youthful energy.

**A** **PAIR WORK** Match the questions and responses. Then ask and answer the questions. Respond using a complex noun phrase followed by a gerund.

**Questions**

1. What's the most challenging thing about working from home? ............
2. What's the best thing about being a police officer? ............
3. What's one of the rewards of being a teacher? ............
4. What's one of the most difficult things about being an emergency-room nurse? ............
5. What's one of the most interesting aspects of working abroad? ............
6. What's one of the most difficult aspects of doing volunteer work? ............
7. What's the hardest part about being overseas? ............

**Responses**

a. dealing with life-or-death situations every day
b. finding enough time to do it on a regular basis
c. learning how people in other cultures live and think
d. helping people learn things that they couldn't learn on their own
e. not talking with my family regularly
f. getting to know people from all parts of society
g. not being distracted by household chores or hobbies

A: What's the most challenging thing about working from home?
B: The most challenging thing about working from home is not being distracted by household chores or hobbies.

**B** **GROUP WORK** Ask the questions in part A again and answer with your own ideas.

## 4 PRONUNCIATION *Stress and rhythm*

**A** ▶ Listen and practice. Notice how stressed words and syllables occur with a regular rhythm.

●       ●       ●       ●

The most rewarding thing │ about traveling │ is learning │ about other cultures.

●       ●       ●       ●       ●

The most frustrating thing │ about working │ in a foreign country │ is missing │ friends and family.

**B** **PAIR WORK** Take turns reading the sentences in the grammar box in Exercise 3. Pay attention to stress and rhythm.

## 5 INTERCHANGE 16 *Viewpoints*

Take a survey about volunteering. Go to Interchange 16 on page 131.

## 6 LISTENING *Challenges and rewards*

▶ Listen to these people talk about their work. What is the biggest challenge of each person's job? What is the greatest reward? Complete the chart.

|  | Biggest challenge | Greatest reward |
|---|---|---|
| 1. psychologist | | |
| 2. camp counselor | | |
| 3. firefighter | | |

## 7 WORD POWER *Antonyms*

**A** Complete the pairs of opposites with the words in the box. Then compare with a partner.

| compassionate | cynical | dependent | rigid | timid | unimaginative |
|---|---|---|---|---|---|

1. adaptable ≠ .........................................
2. courageous ≠ .........................................
3. insensitive ≠ .........................................
4. resourceful ≠ .........................................
5. self-sufficient ≠ .........................................
6. upbeat ≠ .........................................

**B** GROUP WORK How many words or things can you associate with each word in part A?

A: What words or things do you associate with *adaptable*?
B: Flexible.
C: Easy to get along with.

## 8 DISCUSSION *Rewarding work*

**GROUP WORK** What are the special challenges and rewards of working in these situations? Would you ever consider working in one of these areas? Why or why not?

working with animals
teaching gifted children
cooking food at a homeless shelter
working for a nonprofit organization
working in a home for the visually impaired

A: I suppose the most challenging thing about working with animals is . . .
B: But one of the rewards of working with animals must be . . .

## 9 CONVERSATION *I've managed to get good grades, but . . .*

**A** ▶ Listen and practice.

Uncle Ed: Happy birthday, Alison! So how does it feel to be 21?

Alison: Kind of strange. I suddenly feel a little anxious, like I'm not moving ahead fast enough.

Uncle Ed: But don't you think you've accomplished quite a bit in the last few years?

Alison: Oh, I've managed to get good grades, but I still haven't been able to decide on a career.

Uncle Ed: Well, what do you hope you'll have achieved by the time you're 30?

Alison: For one thing, I hope I'll have seen more of the world. But more important than that, I'd like to have made a good start on my career by then.

**B** CLASS ACTIVITY How similar are you to Alison? Are you satisfied with your accomplishments so far? What do you want to accomplish next?

## 10 GRAMMAR FOCUS

> ### Accomplishments and goals ▶
>
> | **Accomplishments with the present perfect or simple past** | **Goals with the future perfect or would like to have + past participle** |
> |---|---|
> | I**'ve managed** to get good grades. (I **managed** to . . . ) I**'ve been able** to accomplish a lot in college. (I **was able** to . . . ) | What do you hope you**'ll have achieved**? I hope I**'ll have seen** more of the world. I**'d like to have made** a good start on my career. |

**A** What are some of your accomplishments from the last five years? Check (✓) the statements that are true for you. Then think of four more statements about yourself.

- ☐ 1. I've met the person who's right for me.
- ☐ 2. I've learned some important life skills.
- ☐ 3. I was able to complete my degree.
- ☐ 4. I've made an important career move.

**B** What are some goals you would like to have accomplished in the future? Complete the sentences.

1. By this time next year, I hope I'll have . . .
2. Three years from now, I'd like to have . . .
3. In ten years, I'd like to have . . .
4. By the time I'm 60, I hope I'll have . . .

**C** GROUP WORK Compare your sentences in parts A and B. What accomplishments do you have in common? What goals?

*Challenges and accomplishments* ▪ **109**

## 11 LISTENING *Future plans*

**A** ▶ Listen to three young people discuss their plans for the future. What do they hope they'll have achieved by the time they are 30?

| 1. Rick | 2. Jasmine | 3. Bianca |
|---------|------------|-----------|
| ............................... | ............................... | ............................... |
| ............................... | ............................... | ............................... |
| ............................... | ............................... | ............................... |

**B** PAIR WORK Who do you think has the most realistic expectations?

## 12 WRITING *A personal statement for an application*

**A** Imagine you are applying to a school or for a job that requires a personal statement. Use these questions to organize your ideas. Make notes and then write a draft.

1. What has your greatest accomplishment been? Has it changed you in any way? How?
2. What are some interesting or unusual facts about yourself that make you a good choice for the job or school?
3. What is something you hope to have achieved ten years from now? When, why, and how will you reach this goal? Will achieving it change you? Why or why not?

> I think my greatest accomplishment has been finally getting my diploma at age 30. I've been able to achieve many things in school with the support of my family, and . . .
>
> There are two things I'd really like to have achieved by the time I'm 40. First, I hope I'll have done some traveling. . . .

**B** GROUP WORK Share your statements and discuss each person's accomplishments and goals. Who has the most unusual accomplishment or goal? the most realistic? the most ambitious?

# Young and Gifted

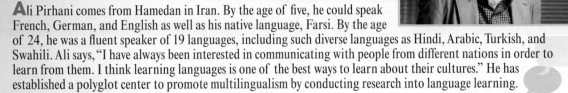

*Scan the article. Who is happy to spend lots of time alone? Who is multilingual? Who has done community service?*

**A**li Pirhani comes from Hamedan in Iran. By the age of five, he could speak French, German, and English as well as his native language, Farsi. By the age of 24, he was a fluent speaker of 19 languages, including such *diverse* languages as Hindi, Arabic, Turkish, and Swahili. Ali says, "I have always been interested in communicating with people from different nations in order to learn from them. I think learning languages is one of the best ways to learn about their cultures." He has established a *polyglot* center to promote multilingualism by conducting research into language learning.

**A** lot of people have sailed, nonstop and alone, around the world, but Jessica Watson claims to be the first 16-year-old to have done so. On May 15, 2010, she returned to Sydney, Australia, after 210 days at sea. However, her claim is not recognized by the World Sailing Speed Record Council. As its name suggests, the council only considers speed records, not factors such as age. Also, the council's minimum distance to qualify for *circumnavigation* is 26,000 nautical miles, but Jessica's route, via the southern oceans, was shorter than this. Her reaction to the council's decision? "It really doesn't bother me."

**A**t age 10, Samson Diamond joined a music project in Soweto, South Africa, and picked up a violin. He soon became leader of the project's Buskaid Soweto String Ensemble, which plays classical music. Later, he obtained a master's degree in music performance. He has also used his talent to serve poor communities in England, Jamaica, and his home country by teaching underprivileged people how to empower themselves through music. He says, "My philosophy is 'the further you go, the further there is to go. Never stop searching.'"

**A** Read the article. Find the words in *italics* in the article.
Then match each word with its meaning.

|  |  |
|---|---|
| ............ 1. *diverse* | a. sailing (or flying) around something |
| ............ 2. *polyglot* | b. poor, not having the things most people have |
| ............ 3. *circumnavigation* | c. different |
| ............ 4. *underprivileged* | d. speaking or using many different languages |

**B** Which statements are inferences (**I**)? Which are restatements (**R**)?
Which are not given (**NG**)?

............ 1. Ali Pirhani learned a lot of languages when he was a teenager.
............ 2. He believes that culture and language are closely connected.
............ 3. Jessica Watson circumnavigated the world via the southern oceans.
............ 4. She plans to circumnavigate the world via a longer route.
............ 5. Samson Diamond was a fast learner on the violin
............ 6. He wants young people to play sports as well as music.

**C** **GROUP WORK** Which person do you think is making the biggest contribution to society? Why?
What personal characteristics made it possible for him or her to achieve so much?

# Units 15–16 Progress check

## SELF-ASSESSMENT

How well can you do these things? Check (✓) the boxes.

| I can . . . . | Very well | OK | A little |
|---|---|---|---|
| Give recommendations and opinions about rules (Ex. 1) | ☐ | ☐ | ☐ |
| Understand and express opinions, and seek agreement (Ex. 2) | ☐ | ☐ | ☐ |
| Describe qualities necessary to achieve particular goals (Ex. 3) | ☐ | ☐ | ☐ |
| Describe challenges connected with particular goals (Ex. 3) | ☐ | ☐ | ☐ |
| Ask about and describe personal achievements and ambitions (Ex. 4) | ☐ | ☐ | ☐ |

## 1 DISCUSSION  *Setting the rules*

**A** **PAIR WORK**  What kinds of rules do you think should be made for these places? Talk with your partner and make three rules for each. (Have fun! Don't make your rules too serious.)

a health club          an apartment building
a school               the school library

**B** **GROUP WORK**  Join another pair. Share your ideas. Do they agree?

A: People should be required to use every machine in a health club.
B: That sounds interesting. Why?
A: Well, for one thing, people would be in better shape!

## 2 LISTENING  *Social issues*

**A** ▶ Listen to people give opinions. Check (✓) the correct responses.

1. ☐ Yes, it is.
   ☐ Yes, they are.

2. ☐ Yes, they do.
   ☐ Yes, they should.

3. ☐ Yes, we do.
   ☐ Yes, it does.

4. ☐ Yes, it does.
   ☐ Yes, it should.

5. ☐ No, they can't.
   ☐ No, it isn't.

6. ☐ No, they don't.
   ☐ No, you can't.

**B** **PAIR WORK**  Write a tag question for each response you did not check.

> 1. Stray animals are so sad, aren't they? Yes, they are.

## 3 DISCUSSION *What does it take?*

**A** **GROUP WORK** What qualities are good or bad if you want to accomplish these goals? Talk with the group and decide on two qualities for each.

| Goals | Qualities | | |
|---|---|---|---|
| hike across your country | adaptable | dependent | self-sufficient |
| conduct an orchestra | compassionate | insensitive | timid |
| make a low-budget movie | courageous | resourceful | unimaginative |
| become a salsa instructor | cynical | rigid | upbeat |

A: To hike across your country, you need to be courageous.
B: Yeah, and you can't be dependent on anyone.

**B** **GROUP WORK** What do you think would be the most challenging things about achieving the goals in part A? How would you overcome the challenges?

A: I think the most challenging thing about hiking across your country would be feeling lonely all the time.
B: I agree. So how would you cope with loneliness?

## 4 ROLE PLAY *Interview*

*Student A:* Student B is going to interview you for the school website. Think about your accomplishments and goals. Then answer the questions.

*Student B:* Imagine you are interviewing Student A for the school website. Add two questions to the notebook. Then start the interview.

Change roles and try the role play again.

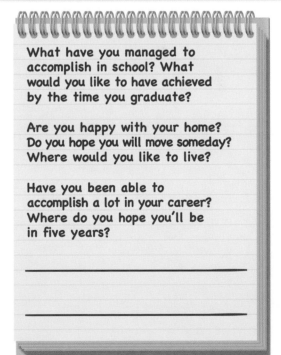

What have you managed to accomplish in school? What would you like to have achieved by the time you graduate?

Are you happy with your home? Do you hope you will move someday? Where would you like to live?

Have you been able to accomplish a lot in your career? Where do you hope you'll be in five years?

_____

_____

## WHAT'S NEXT?

Look at your Self-assessment again. Do you need to review anything?

*PUT YOURSELF IN MY SHOES!*

**A** **PAIR WORK** Read these comments made by parents. Why do you think they feel this way? Think of two arguments to support each point of view.

Our daughter wants to get her ears pierced. We think she should wait until she's 16.

Our son wants to get his computer upgraded, but it's not necessary. We just bought it last year!

If our daughter insists on having her nails done, she has to pay for it herself.

Our son wants to buy a motorcycle. He has the money, but we feel he should save it for college.

Our daughter wants to go to a rock concert with her friends. Absolutely not!

Our son wants to have his hair cut at an expensive salon. What's wrong with a regular barber?

Regardless of the color, we refuse to let our kids get their hair dyed.

A: Why do you think they won't let their daughter get her ears pierced?
B: They probably think she's too young.
A: They may also feel that she . . .

**B** **PAIR WORK** Now put yourselves in the children's shoes. One of you is the daughter and the other is the son. Discuss the parents' decisions, and think of two arguments against their point of view.

A: Why do you think mom and dad won't let me get my ears pierced?
B: They probably think you're too young.
A: That's crazy! My friend got her ears pierced when she was 10. It's not a big deal.

**C** **CLASS ACTIVITY** Take a vote. Do you agree with the parents or the children? Why?

## Student A

**A** **PAIR WORK** Ask your partner these questions. Put a check (✓) if your partner gives the correct answer. (The correct answers are in **bold**.)

2000 Sydney Olympics

3D movie from the 1950s

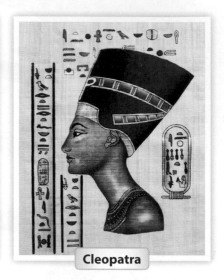

Cleopatra

# Test Your Knowledge ✓

1. Was Julius Caesar emperor of Athens, **Rome**, or Constantinople?

2. What did Thomas Edison invent in 1879? Was it the television, the telephone, or the **lightbulb**?

3. In which year did Mexico gain its independence? Was it in 1721, **1821**, or 1921?

4. Where were the 2000 Olympics held? Were they in Athens, **Sydney**, or Beijing?

5. When did World War I take place? Was it from 1898 to 1903, from 1911 to 1915, or **from 1914 to 1918**?

6. What sculptor made the famous statue of David? Was it Leonardo da Vinci, Auguste Bartholdi, or **Michelangelo**?

7. Who was the first human in space? Was it **Yuri Gagarin**, Neil Armstrong, or John Glenn?

8. When were the first audio CDs put on the market? Was it in 1973, **1983**, or 1993?

9. In what decade did 3-D movies first gain wide popularity? Was it the **1950s**, 1960s, or 1970s?

10. Was Cleopatra the queen of **Egypt**, Rome, or Greece?

**B** **PAIR WORK** Answer the questions your partner asks you. Then compare quizzes. Who has the most correct answers?

**C** **CLASS ACTIVITY** Think of three more questions of your own. Can the rest of the class answer them?

# *WHEN I WAS YOUNGER,...*

**A PAIR WORK** Play the board game. Follow these instructions.

1. Use small pieces of paper with your initials on them as markers.
2. Take turns by tossing a coin:

 **Heads** Move two spaces.　　　 **Tails** Move one space.

3. When you land on a space, tell your partner what is true. Then say how things would have been different. For example:

"When I was younger, I didn't pay attention in class. If I had paid attention in class, I would have gotten better grades."
OR
"When I was younger, I paid attention in class. If I hadn't paid attention in class, I wouldn't have won a scholarship."

**B CLASS ACTIVITY** Who was sensible when they were younger? Who was rebellious? Tell the class.

## Student B

**A** **PAIR WORK** Answer the questions your partner asks you.

**B** **PAIR WORK** Ask your partner these questions. Put a check (✓) if your partner gives the correct answer. (The correct answers are in **bold**.) Then compare quizzes. Who has the most correct answers?

**The Wright Brothers**

**Mary Shelley's *Frankenstein***

**Hong Kong, 1997**

# Test Your Knowledge

1. When did the Wright brothers make their first airplane flight? Was it in 1893, **1903**, or 1923?

2. What was the former name of New York City? Was it New England, New London, or **New Amsterdam**?

3. When did Walt Disney make his first cartoon movie? Was it in 1920, **1938**, or 1947?

4. In which century did the composer Mozart live? Was it the seventeenth, **eighteenth**, or nineteenth century?

5. Who was the novel *Frankenstein* written by? Was it Jane Austen, John Keats, or **Mary Shelley**?

6. Who discovered penicillin? Was it **Alexander Fleming**, Marie Curie, or Albert Einstein?

7. When was the first Volkswagen "Beetle" car built? Was it during the 1920s, the **1930s**, or the 1940s?

8. Who used the first magnetic compass? Was it the Portuguese, **the Chinese**, or the Dutch?

9. When did the British return Hong Kong to China? Was it in 1995, 1996, or **1997**?

10. Was the theory of relativity created by **Albert Einstein**, Charles Darwin, or Isaac Newton?

**C** **CLASS ACTIVITY** Think of three more questions of your own. Can the rest of the class answer them?

**A PAIR WORK** Read these popular slogans for products.
Match the slogans with the product types.

1. It's the real thing. ............
2. The happiest place on earth ............
3. Good to the last drop ............
4. All the news that's fit to print ............
5. Just do it! ............
6. Bet you can't eat just one. ............

a. an amusement park
b. a soft drink
c. coffee
d. a daily newspaper
e. potato chips
f. sports clothing

7. You're in good hands. ............
8. Reach out and touch someone. ............
9. Alarmed? You should be. ............
10. M'm! M'm! Good! ............
11. Built for the road ahead ............
12. Have it your way. ............

g. fast food
h. automobiles
i. security systems
j. insurance
k. soup
l. telephone service

**B PAIR WORK** Join another pair and compare your answers.
Then check your answers at the bottom of the page.

**C GROUP WORK** Think of a product. Then create your
own slogan for it and add a logo. Consider a design
and colors that are suitable for the product.

A: Any idea for a product?
B: What about a pizza delivery service?
C: That's good. Let's try to think of some catchy slogans.
D: How about "Delicious and dependable"? Or maybe . . .

**D CLASS ACTIVITY** Present your slogans to the class.
Who has the catchiest one?

Answers: 1. b; 2. a; 3. c; 4. d; 5. f; 6. e; 7. j; 8. l; 9. i; 10. k; 11. h; 12. g

**A** **PAIR WORK** Look at these pictures. What do you think might have happened in each situation? Talk about possibilities for each picture.

A: Maybe the woman thought of something funny that had happened earlier.

B: Or, she might not have understood . . .

<table>
<tr><td>useful expressions</td></tr>
<tr><td>
Maybe he/she was . . . when . . .<br>
Or perhaps he/she was . . .<br>
He/She may have . . . when . . .<br>
He/She might have . . .
</td></tr>
</table>

1

2

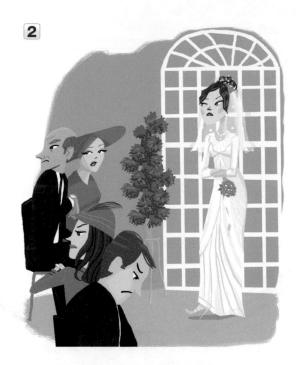

3

4

**B** **GROUP WORK** Agree on one interpretation of each situation and share it with the class. Be ready to answer any questions.

**A** **GROUP WORK** Here are some additional jobs in the movie industry.
What do you think each person does?

| | | | |
|---|---|---|---|
| art director | costume designer | makeup artist | sound-effects technician |
| cinematographer | lighting technician | set designer | special-effects designer |

A: What does an art director do?
B: I know. An art director manages the people who build the sets.

**B** **GROUP WORK** Imagine you are going to make a movie. What kind of
movie will it be? Decide what job each person in your group will do.

A: You should be the art director because you're a good leader.
B: Actually, I'd prefer to be the producer.
C: I think I'd like to be one of the actors.

**C** **CLASS ACTIVITY** Tell the class what kind of movie you are going to make.
Explain how each person will contribute to the making of the film.

a cinematographer

a makeup artist

a lighting technician

a sound-effects technician

**A PAIR WORK** What punishment (if any) is appropriate for each possible offense? Complete the chart.

| Offense | Punishment |
|---|---|
| 1. failing to clean up after a dog | ............................................... |
| 2. crossing the street in dangerous places | ............................................... |
| 3. leaving trash on public streets | ............................................... |
| 4. using a cell phone while driving | ............................................... |
| 5. buying pirated DVDs and video games | ............................................... |
| 6. driving without a seat belt | ............................................... |
| 7. riding a motorcycle without a helmet | ............................................... |
| 8. painting graffiti on public property | ............................................... |
| 9. stealing from your company | ............................................... |
| 10. shoplifting | ............................................... |
| 11. hacking into a government computer | ............................................... |
| 12. ........................................ (your own idea) | ............................................... |

A: What do you think should be done about people who don't clean up after their dogs?
B: They should be required to pay a fine.
A: I don't agree. I think . . .

**possible punishments**

receive a warning
spend some time in jail
pay a fine
lose a driver's license
get suspended
do community service

**B GROUP WORK** Join another pair of students. Then compare and discuss your lists. Do you agree or disagree? Try to convince each other that you are right!

**A** Complete this survey with your viewpoints on communities, charities, and volunteering.

## WHAT DO YOU THINK?

**1** **Do you help out in your community?**
- ☐ Yes, I do regularly.
- ☐ Yes, I do from time to time.
- ☐ No, I don't right now.
- ☐ other: _____

**2** **Would you consider working in a developing country?**
- ☐ Yes. It would be an interesting experience.
- ☐ Maybe when I'm older.
- ☐ No. That's definitely not for me.
- ☐ other: _____

**3** **What's the best way to raise money for charities?**
- ☐ through donations
- ☐ through taxes
- ☐ through special fund-raising activities
- ☐ other: _____

**4** **Who do you think has the greatest responsibility to support charities?**
- ☐ the government
- ☐ all citizens
- ☐ the wealthy
- ☐ other: _____

**5** **What's the best way to improve a community?**
- ☐ through education
- ☐ by creating more jobs
- ☐ by protecting the environment
- ☐ other: _____

**6** **Which of these things are you most concerned about?**
- ☐ the environment
- ☐ crime and safety
- ☐ unemployment
- ☐ other: _____

**7** **Which of these activities would you prefer doing?**
- ☐ helping the elderly
- ☐ helping the poor
- ☐ helping the sick
- ☐ other: _____

**8** **What advice would you give someone who wanted to work for a charitable organization?**
- ☐ Go for it! It can be very rewarding.
- ☐ Be selective about who you decide to work for.
- ☐ Don't do it. It's a waste of time.
- ☐ other: _____

**B** **PAIR WORK** Compare your responses. Do you and your partner have similar viewpoints?

**C** **CLASS ACTIVITY** Take a class poll. Which choice was the most popular for each question? Talk about any "other" responses people added.

# Grammar plus

## Unit 9

### 1 Get or have something done (page 59)

▶ Sentences with *get/have* + object + past participle are passive. BUT Don't use any form of *be* before the past participle: Where can I **have** my watch **fixed**? (NOT: Where can I have my watch ~~be~~ fixed?)

Rewrite the statements as questions with *Where can I get/have . . . ?* Then complete B's answers with the information in parentheses.

1. I want to have someone shorten this skirt.
   A: Where can I have this skirt shortened?
   B: You can have it shortened at Cathy's Cleaners. (at Cathy's Cleaners)
2. I need to get someone to repair my computer.
   A: .................................................................................
   B: ................................................................................. (at Hackers Inc.)
3. I need to have someone prepare my taxes.
   A: .................................................................................
   B: ................................................................................. (by my accountant)
4. I'd like to get someone to cut my hair.
   A: .................................................................................
   B: ................................................................................. (at Beauty Barn)
5. I need to have someone paint my apartment.
   A: .................................................................................
   B: ................................................................................. (by Peter the Painter)

### 2 Making suggestions (page 61)

▶ Use the base form of a verb – without *to* – after *Maybe you could . . .* and *Why don't you . . . ?*: Maybe you could **join** a book club. (NOT: Maybe you could ~~to~~ join a book club.) Why don't you **join** a book club? (NOT: Why don't you ~~to~~ join a book club?)

Complete the conversations with the correct form of the verbs in parentheses.

A: I'm having trouble meeting people here in the city. Any ideas?
B: I know it's hard. Why don't you ......join...... (join) a gym? That's usually a good place to meet people. Or maybe you could ..................... (take) a class at the community college.
A: What about ............................... (check out) the personal ads? Do you think that's a good way to meet people?
B: I wouldn't recommend doing that. People never tell the truth in those ads. But it might be a good idea ............................... (find) a sports team. Have you thought about ............................... (play) a team sport – maybe baseball or volleyball?
A: I'm not very good at most sports, but I used to play tennis.
B: There you go! One option is ............................... (look up) tennis clubs in the city and see which clubs have teams people can join.
A: Now, that's a great idea. And I could always use the exercise!

# Unit 10

## 1 Referring to time in the past (page 65)

> ▶ Use *since* with a particular time: The UN has been in existence **since** 1945. Use *for* with a duration of time: The UN has been in existence **for** about the last 70 years.
> ▶ Use *in* and *during* with a specific period of time: Rock 'n' roll became popular **in/during** the 1950s.
> ▶ Use *from* and *to* to describe when something began and ended: World War II lasted **from** 1939 **to** 1945.

Complete the conversation with the words in the box. (Use some of the words more than once.)

> ago    during    for    from    in    since    to

A:  Hey, Dad. Did you use to listen to the Beatles?
B:  Of course. In fact, I just listened to one of their records a few days
......*ago*....... . Do you realize that the Beatles' music has influenced
other musicians ..................... over 50 years? They were the greatest!
A:  Well, I just found some interesting information about them. I'll read it
to you: "The Beatles were a well-known British band ..................... the
1960s. They performed together ..................... ten years – .....................
1960 ..................... 1970. ..................... 2003, the Beatles released another
album, even though one of the original members had been dead
..................... 1980 and another had died ..................... 2001. The album
had been recorded ..................... 1969 and was in the studio safe
..................... 34 years before it was released."
B:  That *is* interesting. It's pretty amazing that people have listened
to the Beatles ..................... both the twentieth and the twenty-first
centuries, isn't it?

## 2 Predicting the future with *will* (page 67)

> ▶ In sentences referring to time, the preposition *by* means "not later than." Don't confuse *by* with *within*, which means "some time during." Use *by* with points in time; use *within* with periods of time: **By** 2050, we will have eliminated starvation around the world. (NOT: ~~Within~~ 2050, . . .) **Within** the next five years, people will have invented mobile phone applications for nearly everything! (NOT: ~~By~~ the next five years, . . .)

Circle the correct verb forms to complete the conversation.

A:  What do you think you **will do** / (**will be doing**) five years from now?
B:  I'm not sure. Maybe I **will get** / **will have gotten** married by then.
How about you?
A:  I **will be finishing** / **will have finished** medical school, so I
**will be doing** / **will have done** my internship five years from now.
B:  So you **won't be living** / **won't have lived** around here in five years,
I guess. Where do you think you **will live** / **will have lived**?
A:  Wherever I get my internship.

# Unit 11

## 1 Time clauses (page 73)

▶ Use the past perfect in the main clause with *until* and *by the time*. This shows that one of the past events happened before the other: Until I got my driver's license, I **had** always **taken** public transportation. By the time I got my driver's license, all of my friends **had** already **gotten** theirs.

Circle the correct time expression to complete each sentence.

1. **After /** **Until** I traveled overseas, I hadn't known much about different cultures.
2. **After / Before** I got a full-time job, I had to live on a very limited budget.
3. **By the time / Once** I finished high school, I had already taken three college courses.
4. **As soon as / Before** I left for college, my mother turned my room into her office.
5. **Once / Until** I left home, I realized how much my family meant to me.
6. **By the time / The moment** you have a child, you feel totally responsible for him or her.

## 2 Expressing regret and describing hypothetical situations (page 75)

▶ Conditional sentences describing hypothetical situations often refer to both the present and the past:
If I**'d finished** college, I**'d have** a better job now.
      past                    present
(NOT: If I'd finished college, I'd have had a better job now.)

**A** Write sentences with *should (not) have* to express regret about each person's situation.

1. Sarah was very argumentative with her teacher, so she had to stay after school.
   Sarah shouldn't have been argumentative with her teacher.

2. Ivan didn't save up for a car, so he still has to take public transportation.

   .................................................................................................................

3. Jon was very inactive when he was in college, so he gained a lot of weight.

   .................................................................................................................

4. Lisa didn't stay in touch with her high school classmates, so now she has very few friends.

   .................................................................................................................

5. Tony didn't study Spanish in school, so he's not bilingual now.

   .................................................................................................................

**B** Rewrite your sentences in Exercise A, changing them to hypothetical situations.

1. If Sarah hadn't been argumentative with her teacher, she wouldn't have had to stay after school.

2. .................................................................................................................

   .................................................................................................................

3. .................................................................................................................

   .................................................................................................................

4. .................................................................................................................

   .................................................................................................................

5. .................................................................................................................

   .................................................................................................................

# Unit 12

## 1  Describing purpose (page 79)

> ▶ Don't use *for* immediately before an infinitive: **To have** a successful business, you need a lot of luck. (NOT: ~~For~~ to have a successful business, you need a lot of luck.)

**A**  Complete the sentences with *in order to* or *in order for*.

1.  ......In order for...... a supermarket to succeed, it has to be clean and well organized.
2.  .......................... stay popular, a website needs to be accurate and visually attractive.
3.  .......................... run a profitable furniture store, it's important to advertise on TV.
4.  .......................... a restaurant to stay in business, it needs to have "regulars" – customers that come often.
5.  .......................... establish a successful nail salon, it has to have a convenient location.
6.  .......................... an online business to survive, it's a good idea to have excellent pictures of the merchandise it's selling.

**B**  Rewrite the sentences in Exercise A without *In order*.

1.  ...For a supermarket to succeed, it has to be clean and well organized.......................
2.  ..........................................................................................................
3.  ..........................................................................................................
4.  ..........................................................................................................
5.  ..........................................................................................................
6.  ..........................................................................................................

## 2  Giving reasons (page 81)

> ▶ *Because* and *since* have the same meaning, and they can begin or end a sentence: **Because/Since** the food is always fantastic, Giorgio's is my favorite restaurant. = Giorgio's is my favorite restaurant **because/since** the food is always fantastic.
> ▶ Don't confuse *because* and *because of*. *Because* introduces an adverb clause and is followed by a subject and verb, while *because of* is a preposition and is followed by a noun object: **Because** Giorgio's is so popular, we should get there early. Giorgio's is popular **because of** its food and service.

Circle the correct words to complete the conversation.

A:  I had to go downtown today **because / because of / due to** I needed to mail a package at the post office. **Due to / For / Since** I was only a few blocks from Main Street, I went over to Martin's. Did you know that Martin's has gone out of business? I'm so upset!

B:  That's too bad, but I'm not surprised. A lot of family-owned shops are closing **because / because of / since** the construction of shopping malls.

A:  Yeah, and don't forget about all the megastores that are popping up everywhere. **Because / For / The reason why** people prefer to shop there is to save money. Everyone loves a megastore **because / due to / since** the low prices and the huge selection.

B:  Not me! I loved Martin's **for / since / the reason that** their beautiful clothes and friendly salespeople. When you were there, you almost felt like family. You'll never get that at a megastore!

# Unit 13

## 1 Past modals for degrees of certainty (page 87)

> ▶ Use the past modal *could have* to express possibility. BUT Use *couldn't have* when you are almost 100% sure something is impossible: I suppose he **could have gotten** stuck in traffic, but he **couldn't have forgotten** his own birthday party.

Complete the conversations with past modals *must (not) have, could (not) have,* or *may/might (not) have*. Use the degrees of certainty and the verbs in parentheses. (More than one answer may be possible.)

1. A: Yoko still hasn't called me back.
   B: She ...*might not have gotten*... your message. (it's possible – not get)
2. A: What's wrong with Steven?
   B: Oh, you ............................... the news. His dog ran away. (it's almost certain – not hear)
3. A: I went to see the Larsens today, but they didn't answer the door.
   B: Was their car there? If so, they ............................... in the backyard. (it's possible – be)
4. A: Fabio said he was going to the party last night, but I didn't see him.
   B: Neither did I. He ............................... there then. (it's not possible – not be)
5. A: I can't find my glasses, but I know I had them at work today.
   B: You ............................... them at the office. (it's possible – leave)
6. A: Marc's new car looks really expensive.
   B: Yes, it does. It ............................... a fortune! (it's almost certain – cost)

## 2 Past modals for judgments and suggestions (page 89)

> ▶ In advice with *would have*, the speaker means, "If I were you, . . . ."

Read each situation and choose the corresponding judgment or suggestion for an alternative past action.

**Situation**
1. Sue forgot her boyfriend's birthday. ...*b*...
2. Tim got a speeding ticket. ..........
3. Ruth still hasn't paid me back. ..........
4. Bill lied to us. ..........
5. I spent an hour making Joe dinner, and he didn't even thank me. ..........
6. Carol came over for dinner empty-handed. ..........

**Judgment/Suggestion**
a. I wouldn't have lent her money.
b. She should have put it on her calendar.
c. He should have told the truth.
d. He shouldn't have gone over the limit.
e. She should have brought something.
f. I wouldn't have cooked for him.

# Unit 14

## 1 The passive to describe process (page 93)

> ► The modals *have to* and *need to* must agree with the subject; other modals, like *may be*, have only one form: Each scene **has to/needs to** be filmed from several different angles.

Put the words in the correct order to make sentences.

1. overnight / business / A / started / small / isn't / .
   *A small business isn't started overnight.*

2. to / plan / business / a / written / First, / be / has / .
   ....................................................................................................

3. research / Next, / done / be / market / should / .
   ....................................................................................................

4. needs / competition / to / the / Then / identified / be / .
   ....................................................................................................

5. online / ads / posted / be / Classified / may / .
   ....................................................................................................

6. work / are / employees / be / hired / can / started / the / so / Finally, / .
   ....................................................................................................

## 2 Defining and non-defining relative clauses (page 96)

> ► Use either *who* or *that* in defining relative clauses about people: A set designer is an artist **who/that** makes important contributions to a theater production. BUT Use only *who* in non-defining relative clauses about people: A set designer, **who** makes important contributions to a theater production, has to be very creative. (NOT: A set designer, ~~that~~ makes . . .)
> ► Use commas before and after a non-defining clause: A gossip columnist, who gets to go to fabulous parties, writes about celebrities and scandals.

Combine these sentences with *who* or *that*. Add a comma wherever one is necessary.

1. A prop designer makes sure everything on a movie set looks realistic.
   He or she is good with details.
   *A prop designer, who is good with details, makes sure everything on a movie set looks realistic.*

2. A screenwriter is a talented person. He or she develops a story idea into a movie script.
   *A screenwriter is a talented person that develops a story idea into a movie script.*

3. A script doctor is a writer. He or she is used when a screenplay needs more work.
   ....................................................................................................

4. Casting directors choose an actor for each part in a movie. They have usually been in the movie business for a long time.
   ....................................................................................................

5. High-budget movies always use big stars. The stars are known around the world.
   ....................................................................................................

6. Movie directors are greatly respected. They "make or break" a film.
   ....................................................................................................

# Unit 15

## 1 Giving recommendations and opinions (page 101)

> ▶ *Ought to* has the same meaning as *should*, but it's more formal: Traffic signs **ought to** be obeyed. = Traffic signs **should** be obeyed.

A student committee is discussing rules for their school. Complete speaker B's sentences with appropriate passive modals. (More than one answer is possible.)

1. A: Students must be required to clean off the cafeteria tables after lunch.
   B: I disagree. Students ....*shouldn't be required*.... to do that. That's what the cafeteria workers are paid to do.
2. A: Teachers shouldn't be allowed to park in the student parking lot.
   B: Why not? Teachers ................................................ to park wherever a space is available. After all, they're here for us.
3. A: A rule has to be made to ban the use of cell phones in school.
   B: I don't think a rule ................................................ . Students may need their phones for emergency purposes.
4. A: Students mustn't be permitted to use calculators during math exams.
   B: Sometimes we ................................................ to use them, especially when we're being tested on more complicated concepts than simple arithmetic.
5. A: Something has got to be done to control the noise in the hallways.
   B: Students ................................................ to talk to each other between classes, though. They aren't disturbing anyone when classes aren't in session.
6. A: Teachers must be required to remind students about important exams.
   B: That's unnecessary. On the contrary, students ................................................ to follow the syllabus and check important dates on the course websites.

## 2 Tag questions for opinions (page 103)

> ▶ Tag questions added to statements in the simple present and simple past use the corresponding auxiliary verb in the tag: You **agree** with me, **don't** you? You **don't agree** with me, **do** you? You **paid** the rent, **didn't** you? You **didn't pay** the electric bill, **did** you?

Check (✓) the sentences if the tag questions are correct. If they're incorrect, write the correct tag questions.

1. Food is getting more and more expensive, ~~is it~~? .......*isn't it*.......
2. Supermarkets should try to keep their prices down, shouldn't they? .........✓.........
3. People don't buy as many fresh fruits and vegetables as they used to, do we? ................................
4. We have to buy healthy food for our children, don't we? ................................
5. Many children go to school hungry, won't they? ................................
6. Some people can't afford to eat meat every day, don't they? ................................
7. We can easily live without eating meat every day, can we? ................................
8. A lot of people are having a hard time making ends meet these days, haven't they? ................................

# Unit 16

## 1 Complex noun phrases containing gerunds (page 107)

> ▶ Complex noun phrases usually contain gerunds. Often they are also followed by gerunds: One of the most challenging things about **being** a teacher is **not becoming** impatient with difficult students.
>
> ▶ Different prepositions follow different nouns. Use *about* with *thing(s)*: What's the best thing **about** working from home? BUT Use *of* after *challenge(s)*, *reward(s)* and *aspect(s)*: What's one of the rewards **of** being a social worker? One of the best aspects **of** being a social worker is helping people. NOTE: Use *of* or *about* with *part(s)*: What's the best part **about** being a mom? The best part **of** it is being a witness to your children's lives.

Read each situation. Use the words in parentheses to write a sentence with a noun phrase containing a gerund.

1. I work in an office. (one challenge = getting along with co-workers)
   *One of the challenges of working in an office is getting along with your co-workers.*
2. I have a job abroad. (most difficult thing = dealing with homesickness)
   .................................................................................................
3. I work in a nursing home. (best aspect = helping people feel more positive about life)
   .................................................................................................
4. I work in a rural clinic. (most frustrating part = not having enough supplies)
   .................................................................................................
5. I'm a child-care worker. (one reward = making the children feel safe)
   .................................................................................................

## 2 Accomplishments and goals (page 109)

> ▶ When talking about past accomplishments and including a specific time, use the simple past – not the present perfect: I **was** able to complete my degree last year. (NOT: I've been able to complete my degree last year.)

**A** Complete the sentences about Ana's accomplishments. Use the verbs in parentheses. (More than one answer is possible.)

In the last five years, Ana . . .
1. _managed to finish_ (finish) college.
2. ........................... (pay) all her college loans.
3. ........................... (start) her own company.
4. ........................... (move) to the city.
5. ........................... (make) some new friends.

**B** Complete the sentences about Ana's goals. Use the verbs in parentheses. (More than one answer is possible.)

Five years from now, Ana . . .
1. _would like to have expanded_ (expand) her business.
2. ........................... (meet) the man of her dreams.
3. ........................... (travel) to South America and Asia.
4. ........................... (get) married.
5. ........................... (buy) a house.

# Grammar plus answer key

## Unit 9

### 1  Get or have something done

2.  **A:** Where can I get/have my computer repaired?
    **B:** You can get/have it repaired at Hackers Inc.
3.  **A:** Where can I get/have my taxes prepared?
    **B:** You can get/have them prepared by my accountant.
4.  **A:** Where can I get/have my hair cut?
    **B:** You can get/have it cut at Beauty Barn.
5.  **A:** Where can I get/have my apartment painted?
    **B:** You can get/have it painted by Peter the Painter.

### 2  Making suggestions

**A:** I'm having trouble meeting people here in the city. Any ideas?
**B:** I know it's hard. Why don't you **join** a gym? That's usually a good place to meet people. Or maybe you could **take** a class at the community college.
**A:** What about **checking out** the personal ads? Do you think that's a good way to meet people?
**B:** I wouldn't recommend doing that. People never tell the truth in those ads. But it might be a good idea **to find** a sports team. Have you thought about **playing** a team sport – maybe baseball or volleyball?
**A:** I'm not very good at most sports, but I used to play tennis.
**B:** There you go! One option is **to look up** tennis clubs in the city and see which clubs have teams people can join.
**A:** Now, that's a great idea. And I could always use the exercise!

## Unit 10

### 1  Referring to time in the past

**A:** Hey, Dad. Did you use to listen to the Beatles?
**B:** Of course. In fact, I just listened to one of their records a few days **ago**. Do you realize that the Beatles' music has influenced other musicians **for** over 50 years? They were the greatest!
**A:** Well, I just found some interesting information about them. I'll read it to you: "The Beatles were a well-known British band **during/in** the 1960s. They performed together **for** ten years – **from** 1960 **to** 1970. **In** 2003, the Beatles released another album, even though one of the original members had been dead **since** 1980 and another had died **in** 2001. The album had been recorded **in** 1969 and was in the studio safe **for** 34 years before it was released."
**B:** That is interesting. It's pretty amazing that people have listened to the Beatles **in** both the twentieth and the twenty-first centuries, isn't it?

### 2  Predicting the future with *will*

**A:** What do you think you **will be doing** five years from now?
**B:** I'm not sure. Maybe I **will have gotten** married by then. How about you?

**A:** I **will have finished** medical school, so I **will be doing** my internship five years from now.
**B:** So you **won't be living** around here in five years, I guess. Where do you think you **will live**?
**A:** Wherever I get my internship.

## Unit 11

### 1  Time clauses

2.  Before
3.  By the time
4.  As soon as
5.  Once
6.  The moment

### 2  Expressing regret and describing hypothetical situations

**A**

2.  Ivan should have saved up for a car.
3.  Jon shouldn't have been inactive when he was in college.
4.  Lisa should have stayed in touch with her high school classmates.
5.  Tony should have studied Spanish in school.

**B**

*Answer may vary. Some possible answers:*

2.  If Ivan had saved up for a car, he wouldn't have to take public transportation.
3.  If Jon hadn't been inactive when he was in college, he wouldn't have gained a lot of weight.
4.  If Lisa had stayed in touch with her high school classmates, she wouldn't have very few friends.
5.  If Tony had studied Spanish in school, he would be bilingual now.

## Unit 12

### 1  Describing purpose

**A**

2.  In order to
3.  In order to
4.  In order for
5.  In order to
6.  In order for

**B**

2.  To stay popular, a website needs to be accurate and visually attractive.
3.  To run a profitable furniture store, it's important to advertise on TV.
4.  For a restaurant to stay in business, it needs to have "regulars" – customers that come often.
5.  To establish a successful nail salon, it has to have a convenient location.
6.  For an online business to survive, it's a good idea to have excellent pictures of the merchandise it's selling.

## 2 Giving reasons

A: I had to go downtown today **because** I needed to mail a package at the post office. **Since** I was only a few blocks from Main Street, I went over to Martin's. Did you know that Martin's has gone out of business? I'm so upset!

B: That's too bad, but I'm not surprised. A lot of family-owned shops are closing **because of** the construction of shopping malls.

A: Yeah, and don't forget about all the megastores that are popping up everywhere. **The reason why** people prefer to shop there is to save money. Everyone loves a megastore **due to** the low prices and the huge selection.

B: Not me! I loved Martin's **for** their beautiful clothes and friendly salespeople. When you were there, you almost felt like family. You'll never get that at a megastore!

# Unit 13

## 1 Past modals for degrees of certainty

*Answer may vary. Some possible answers:*

2. A: What's wrong with Steven?
   B: Oh, you **must not have heard** the news. His dog ran away.
3. A: I went to see the Larsens today, but they didn't answer the door.
   B: Was their car there? If so, they **could have been** in the backyard.
4. A: Fabio said he was going to the party last night, but I didn't see him.
   B: Neither did I. He **couldn't have been** there then.
5. A: I can't find my glasses, but I know I had them at work today.
   B: You **might have left** them at the office.
6. A: Marc's new car looks really expensive.
   B: Yes, it does. It **must have cost** a fortune!

## 2 Past modals for judgments and suggestions

2. d    3. a    4. c    5. f    6. e

# Unit 14

## 1 The passive to describe process

2. First, a business plan has to be written.
3. Next, market research should be done.
4. Then the competition needs to be identified.
5. Classified ads may be posted online.
6. Finally, employees are hired so the work can be started.

## 2 Defining and non-defining relative clauses

2. A screenwriter is a talented person who develops a story idea into a movie script.
3. A script doctor is a writer that is used when a screenplay needs more work.
4. Casting directors, who have usually been in the movie business for a long time, choose an actor for each part in a movie.
5. High-budget movies always use big stars that are known around the world.
6. Movie directors, who "make or break" a film, are greatly respected.

# Unit 15

## 1 Giving recommendations and opinions

*Answer may vary. Some possible answers:*

2. A: Teachers shouldn't be allowed to park in the student parking lot.
   B: Why not? Teachers **should be allowed** to park wherever a space is available. After all, they're here for us.
3. A: A rule has to be made to ban the use of cell phones in school.
   B: I don't think a rule **has to be made**. Students may need their phones for emergency purposes.
4. A: Students mustn't be permitted to use calculators during math exams.
   B: Sometimes we **should be permitted** to use them, especially when we're being tested on more complicated concepts than simple arithmetic.
5. A: Something has got to be done to control the noise in the hallways.
   B: Students **should be allowed** to talk to each other between classes, though. They aren't disturbing anyone when classes aren't in session.
6. A: Teachers must be required to remind students about important exams.
   B: That's unnecessary. On the contrary, students **should be required** to follow the syllabus and check important dates on the course websites.

## 2 Tag questions for opinions

3. do they
4. ✓
5. don't they
6. can they
7. can't we
8. aren't they

# Unit 16

## 1 Complex noun phrases containing gerunds

2. The most difficult thing about having a job abroad is dealing with homesickness.
3. The best aspect of working in a nursing home is helping people feel more positive about life.
4. The most frustrating part about/of working in a rural clinic is not having enough supplies.
5. One reward of being a child-care worker is making the children feel safe.

## 2 Accomplishments and goals

*Answer may vary. Some possible answers:*

**A**
2. has managed to pay
3. has been able to start
4. was able to move
5. managed to make

**B**
2. will have met
3. will have traveled
4. would like to have gotten
5. would like to have bought

# Credits

## Illustrations

Jessica Abel: 119, 120; **Andrezzinho:** 87, 94; **Mark Collins:** v;
**Carlos Diaz:** 24 (*top*); **Jada Fitch:** 5 (*bottom*), 25, 64 (*bottom*), 109, 122;
**Tim Foley:** 76; **Travis Foster:** 14, 18, 95 (*right*), 105 (*center*), 117;
**Chuck Gonzales:** 2 (*bottom*), 6, 33, 52, 72 (*bottom*), 103, 128;
**Jim Haynes:** 11, 61; **Dan Hubig:** 125; **Trevor Keen:** 5 (*top*), 75, 83, 102;
**KJA-artists:** 29, 68, 88 (*bottom*); **Shelton Leong:** 47; **Karen Minot:** 2
(*top*), 16 (*top*), 36 (*bottom*), 49, 63, 72 (*top*), 86 (*top*), 95 (*left*), 105, 117
(*background*); **Jeff Moores:** 59; **Rob Schuster:** 8 (*top*), 23, 24 (*bottom*), 32,
56, 58 (*bottom*), 78 (*bottom*), 92, 100, 113, 115 (*bottom*),121, 131;

**Daniel Vasconcellos:** 28, 36 (*top*), 43, 44 (*bottom*), 67, 91 (*top right*),
96, 99, 101; **Brad Walker:** 16 (*bottom*); **Sam Whitehead:** 10, 20, 21 (*center*),
38, 39, 86 (*bottom*), 115 (*top*); **Jeff Wong:** 30; **James Yamasaki:** 19, 79,
88 (*top*), 112, 123, 130; **Rose Zgodzinski:** 7, 13, 22 (*top*), 27, 40, 44
(*top*), 55, 62 (*bottom*), 64 (*top*), 66, 77, 97, 100, 111, 124, 126;
**Carol Zuber-Mallison:** 21 (*top*), 22 (*bottom*), 34, 35, 41, 50 (*top*), 57,
58 (*top*), 69, 78 (*top*), 91, 106 (*top*), 114, 118

## Photos

**4** (*middle right*) © Ariel Skelley/Photographer's Choice/Getty Images;
(*bottom right*) © Smart Creatives/Flame/Corbis
**8** © Douglas Graham/Roll Call Photos/Newscom
**9** (*right, top to bottom*) © OtnaYdur/Shutterstock; © Morgan Lane
Photography/Shutterstock; © Ablestock.com/Getty Images/Thinkstock;
© Slaven/Shutterstock
**12** (*middle, left to right*) ©Tetra Images/Alamy; © Bob Daemmrich/Alamy;
© fStop/SuperStock
**13** (*left, top to bottom*) © Exactostock/SuperStock; © iStockphoto/
Thinkstock; © Exactostock/SuperStock; © Rui Vale de Sousa/Shutterstock;
© Andres Rodriguez/Alamy; © Perfect Pictures/FogStock/Alamy
**15** (*bottom right*) © ester22/Alamy; © Hill Street Studios/Blend Images
**17** © Andy Ryan/The Image Bank/Getty Images
**19** © sozaijiten/Datacraft/Getty Images
**22** ©Tim Laman/National Geographic Stock
**23** © Ocean Image Photography/Shutterstock
**26** © Tanya Constantine/Blend Images/Getty Images
**27** © Michael Caulfield/WireImage/Getty Images
**30** © Travelscape Images/Alamy
**31** © Ian Cumming/Axiom Photographic Agency/Getty Images
**32** © Meeyoung Son/Alamy
**34** (*middle left*) © Dana White/PhotoEdit; (*bottom left*) © Bill Bachman/
Alamy
**35** © Hemis.fr/SuperStock
**37** (*bottom, left to right*) © Craig Dingle/iStockphoto; © Jeffrey Hamilton/
Stockbyte/Thinkstock; © Michael Wells/Getty Images; © Epoxydude/
Getty Images
**40** © ewg3D/iStockphoto
**41** (*bottom, left to right*) © Don Farrall/Photodisc/Getty Images;
© Andy Crawford/Dorling Kindersley/Getty Images; (*lamp*) © Courtesy
of Khader Humied/Metaform Studio; (*coffee table*) © Courtesy of
Joel Hester/The Weld House; © Suzanne Long/Alamy
**42** © arabianEye/Getty Images
**43** © Hemera/Thinkstock
**44** © inga spence/Alamy
**45** (*middle, clockwise*) © Lincoln Rogers/Shutterstock; © luoman/
iStockphoto; © Tim Roberts Photography/Shutterstock; © UNEP/Still
Pictures/The Image Works; © Mark Leach/Alamy; © Barnaby Chambers/
Shutterstock
**46** © Phil Crean A/Alamy
**48** (*top, left to right*) © Bob Daemmrich/The Image Works;
© altrendo images/Getty Images; © JK Enright/Alamy; (*middle right*)
© Joel Stettenheim/Corbis
**49** © Travel Pix/Alamy
**50** © Jack Sullivan/Alamy
**51** (*middle right*) © Science Photo Library/Alamy; (*bottom right*)
© Diego Cervo/Shutterstock
**53** © Bailey-Cooper Photography 4/Alamy
**54** (*top right*) © Bob Ebbesen/Alamy; (*bottom right*) © Hans Martens/
iStockphoto
**55** © Blue Jean Images/Alamy
**57** © Image Source/Corbis
**60** © Eddie Linssen/Alamy
**62** (*middle, left to right*) © Juanmonino/iStockphoto; © Paul Ridsdale/
Alamy; © Chris Rout/Alamy
**63** ©Tetra Images/Getty Images
**64** (*top, left to right*) © Teenage doll/Alamy; © Selyutina Olga/
Shutterstock; © Hemera/Thinkstock; © Stan Honda/AFP/Getty Images/
Newscom; © Hachette Book Group. Used by permission. All rights
reserved. © Reisig and Taylor/ABC/Getty Images
**65** (*top right*) © Handout/MCT/Newscom; (*middle right*) © De Agostini/
SuperStock

**66** © Chung Sung-Jun/Getty Images
**69** © David Livingston/Getty Images
**70** © Image Source/Corbis
**71** (*top right*) © Al Grillo/ZUMA Press/Corbis; (*bottom right*)
© Maisant Ludovic/Hemis/Alamy
**73** © Ariwasabi/Shutterstock
**74** © Gene Chutka/iStockphoto
**77** (*top, left to right*) © El Sebou' - Egyptian Birth Ritual (1986) by
Fadwa El Guindi. Image courtesy of Documentary Educational Resources;
© Jeremy Woodhouse/Blend Images/Alamy; © James Strachan/
Robert Harding Picture Library Ltd/Alamy
**80** (*top right*) © rudy k/Alamy; (*bottom right*) © Ethan Miller/Getty Images
**81** © Ethan Miller/Getty Images
**84** © Image Source/SuperStock
**85** © Max Montecinos/LatinContent/Getty Images
**86** © Elena Elisseeva/Shutterstock
**89** © iStockphoto/Thinkstock
**92** © Macpherson/Prahl/Splash News/Newscom
**93** (*middle right*) © Corbis Bridge/Alamy; (*bottom right*) © Bill Aron/
PhotoEdit
**94** © Myrleen Ferguson Cate/PhotoEdit
**97** © DreamPictures/Taxi/Getty Images
**99** (*top left*) © David Young-Wolff/PhotoEdit; (*top right*) © iStockphoto/
Thinkstock
**100** (*top left*) © Joao Virissimo/Shutterstock; (*top right*) © Gillian Price/
Alamy
**102** © Greg Balfour Evans/Alamy
**104** © B.O'Kane/Alamy
**106** (*top, left to right*) © Getty Images/Photos.com/Thinkstock;
© Daniel Jones/Alamy; © Design Pics/Newscom
**108** (*bottom right*) © Mike Greenlar/Syracuse Newspapers/The Image
Works
**109** © Payless Images, Inc./Alamy
**110** (*top, left to right*) © Rui Vale de Sousa/Shutterstock; © leolintang/
Shutterstock; © Carl Stewart/Alamy
**111** (*top right*) © Courtesy of Ali Pirhani (*middle left*) © AP Photo/
Rob Griffith; (*middle right*) © Gallo Images/Getty Images
**113** © Maridav/iStockphoto
**116** (*top, left to right*) © Kayros Studio Be Happy/Shutterstock; © Karkas/
Shutterstock; © Jovan Svorcan/Shutterstock; (*middle, left to right*)
© Klaus Mellenthin/Westend61/Alloy/Corbis; © Stacie Stauff Smith
Photography/Shutterstock; © iStockphoto/Thinkstock; (*bottom, left to
right*) © Zedcor Wholly/PhotoObjects.net/Thinkstock; © Ragnarock/
Shutterstock; © Alaettin Yildirim/Shutterstock
**118** (*top, left to right*) © Webphotographer/iStockphoto;
© Stuart O'Sullivan/Fancy/Corbis; © BananaStock/Thinkstock
**121** (*middle, left to right*) © AP Photo/Joshua Trujillo; © David Bacon/
Alamy; © Directphoto.org/Alamy
**124** (*top, left to right*) © Hauke Dressler/LOOK Die Bildagentur der
Fotografen GmbH/Alamy; © J. R. Eyerman//Time Life Pictures/Getty
Images; © ewg3D/iStockphoto
**126** (*top, left to right*) © Library of Congress; © Heritage Images/Corbis;
©AP Photo/Pool
**125** © Jeffrey Kuan/iStockphoto
**127** (*bottom, clockwise*) © Don Nichols/iStockphoto; © Martin Thomas
Photography/Alamy; © Evox Productions/Drive Images/Alamy;
© Daniel Bendjy/iStockphoto
**129** (*middle, left to right*) © Exactostock/SuperStock; © Hans Gutknecht/
ZUMA Press/Newscom; (*bottom, left to right*) © Jeff Greenberg/Alamy;
© Michael Newman/PhotoEdit